LIVING WATER TO A THIRSTY LAND

RIVERS OF LIVING WATER

ALAN J. CLARREDGE

ISBN: 9798736923489

To my wife Lilian and all the faithful workers and supporters during the past thirty-six years.

"It is a most engaging story of his experience of God's faithful love and support in his calling. Alan's joy and hope and humour shine out of the writing, and also his patient endurance and constant trust in God throughout all the difficulties and challenges he has faced."

- Dr John Sentamu, Archbishop of York

CONTENTS

FOREWORD

Charles Prince Aerodrome Harare Zimbabwe

Twenty years ago when I first wrote a small book on the work of 'Rivers of Living Water', I never realised that I would still be carrying out work in Africa up to the year two thousand and twenty-one and hopefully beyond.

When God called me for this work He certainly proved to me that He knew what He was doing.

I start this story with no apology for repeating the episode in wartime Mozambique that my first book described, and the incident that gave the name 'Rivers of Living Water' for our African work.

The charity has continued over the years to carry out its work in supplying help for the practical and spiritual needs of the people in the southern hemisphere.

"*Standing transfixed, I was amazed by the large number of small planes leaving the main runway on this, the second largest private aerodrome in central Zimbabwe. My thoughts regarding my sanity, to say the least, were somewhat confused, wondering if in the first place, I had been right to put myself in the predicament that I now found myself in.*

It was February 1987 and whilst attempting to collect my thoughts, the warm fragrant summer air wafted up from the strangely discoloured tarmacadam beneath my feet, its stench catching my nostrils with a heady mixture of hot gasoline and flowering hibiscus shrubs. Cooled only a little by a southern breeze, skimming across the runway from the golden low veldt which stretched out for many miles.

The pollen in the air gently irritated my nose, causing the odd sneeze or two, the slight, but almost imperceptible temperature difference was just enough to give me goose bumps between the turn ups of my shorts and the high woollen khaki socks, that I was wearing, in fact the traditional leg wear worn in central southern Africa since the early 1800s my stocking tops were neatly turned over in the same way I recollect as a school boy growing up during the nineteen forties and the early nineteen fifties.

The goose pimples may have been caused by other reasons, for I was standing with my right thumb raised in the air, waving it to and fro in the time-honoured way of thumbing a lift!

Feeling not a little embarrassed I asked myself what idiot would try to get a plane to stop and give me a lift to a land totally embroiled in Civil War? That idiot was me."

PROLOGUE

As I stood and observed the numberless flowering Jacaranda trees that filled the avenues of Harare, the Capital of Zimbabwe, with their translucent blue haze; my mind boggled at what could only be described as nothing less than an abundance of sheer beauty. Encapsulated by the spectacle, I stood motionless for a good five minutes, gazing upon their magnificence, I felt sure that any visitor like myself on seeing this stunning sight would find it difficult not to be distracted from the present failings and disappointments of the countries new independent political system.

Unfortunately, common sense told me that this diversion from reality could only provide a temporary respite for the inhabitants of the city.

The lack of goods on the supermarket shelves demonstrated that the shops were rapidly becoming devoid of many of the essential household items, such as soap, toothpaste, and in some cases even bread and milk.

The increasing frustrations of searching for such goods completely overshadowed the daily lives of the population. I felt it was sad, coming so soon after the euphoric welcoming of independence from Britain.

*

My accommodation in the early days of my residency depended on the generosity of my new found friends and in turn their friends, those good folks whom I had come to know within the first year or so of my visiting this beautiful ex-colonial country. The nation had been previously known, as Southern Rhodesia, in fact since 1923, when the name was given in honour of Cecil Rhodes. Today a name associated with dubious racial and colonial intentions.

Now after a fierce struggle for independence it had rightfully become a state in its own right, proudly known as, '*The Republic of Zimbabwe*' and geographically set in the heart of central Southern Africa.

Southern Rhodesia

Republic of Zimbabwe

It is with a feeling of great nostalgia that I write this biographical story of my work in Africa, especially when I reminisce over some of the incidents that changed my life and taught me to believe and respect that, ***WITH GOD NOTHING IS IMPOSSIBLE***.

It was July and midwinter in Zimbabwe, not winter as I had experienced in Europe, but for me, after a short period of acclimatization and blood thinning, far too cold for comfort.

Now after staying in a number of dingy and bug-ridden downtown hotels, I was only too pleased to accept temporary accommodation in an empty flat, whilst its owner, a white reporter working for the *Herald* a Zimbabwean national newspaper, had been sent down south to Johannesburg, to cover a large number of important press releases. These significant political announcements currently covered the looming death of apartheid, and hopefully, as far as I was concerned, would last for a further month or two, until I was due to return to the UK.

Housesitting was a good way of cutting down on costs, and of course relief from the poor accommodation that I have just written about.

I well remember the night that I now share with you, for after eating my evening meal in the nearby Wimpy snack bar at the Avondale shopping centre I returned to the reasonably comfortable flat in my hired car and prepared for an early night.

The July weather that particular year had been unusually cold and certainly quite uncomfortable, this was mainly due to the high geographical location of Harare, and quite noticeably the city could be quite icy. Now with the extremely cold airflow from South Africa we were experiencing an extremely low evening temperature.

Shivering, I was forced to lie under the thin apology for a duvet on my bed; this covering did little to alleviate the cold, yet the bed was still the warmest place in the cold room. I had little choice, for prior to getting into the bed I had carried out a very thorough exploration of his cupboards in a fruitless attempt to discover a heater of some sort.

Once I had warmed a little, I turned on the radio and enjoyed listening to a thriller on Zimbabwe radio one, produced by Colin Harvey, whom I got to know during my time in Harare and in fact produced one of my short stories for broadcasting on ZBC. (*Zimbabwean Broadcasting Corporation*). Surprisingly, I became lost in the programme; in fact so relaxed that I fell asleep missing the end of what should have been a first class, '*who dun it*'.

Now once again, having woken up in the draughty room, long after the programme had concluded, I carried out an even more comprehensive investigation of my host's cupboards in the hope I may have missed some form of covering. Unfortunately, as in the case of the heater, and with very little surprise, I drew a total blank for they were completely bare of any blankets, although I remember thinking at the time, that if there had been a step ladder, I could have reached the curtains to take them down, and they would have helped. As it was, I was forced to snuggle beneath the extremely well-worn, wafer thin bedspread which I firmly wrapped, a couple of times around my body.

Normally for most of the year I would have slept on top of the bed, not so on this occasion, for the biting cold forced me to remain tightly ensconced inside my threadbare cover throughout the night.

Somewhat miraculously I had managed to return to sleep quite soundly, even though the large, iron framed old-fashioned bed with its thin and bumpy worn-out mattress offered very little encouragement to rest. As if this hadn't been enough, once under the cover, I had all too quickly discovered a great number of uncomfortable exposed springs, whose sharp edges did very little to assist my repose.

Quite logically any one of these items should have kept me awake, it didn't.

The blast contained within the confined space of my bedroom had to have been deafening to say the very least. In fact as I mulled over the event sometime later, I came to the conclusion that the explosion should have been loud enough to wake the dead, although in my case I have to admit it didn't wake me. I drew this assumption after looking at my watch and comparing it with the clock that had fallen from the wall, I clearly noticed the time on its dial when it had ceased to work.

I quickly observed that quite a few minutes had passed between the incident and my waking up upon the bedroom floor. In fact it took several more minutes before the cause and the position I now found myself in became painfully apparent.

My friends flat, was situated on the first floor of a fairly modern building and was situated in Prince Edward street in a very nice area on the outskirts of the city not far from Belvedere with its large and prestigious golf club, sadly at that time only affordable for the rich, and these being mainly the affluent white residents, probably stirring up resentment.

My peaceful sleep had certainly been shattered by the sudden change of my sleeping arrangements, for having been so rudely woken up. I was left in total confusion. The main reason behind this utter turmoil, was my bed, for it had shifted by at least ten feet, and was now on the opposite wall from where it had been the night before.

Its re-location must have been with sufficient force to throw me onto the threadbare partly carpeted floor of the bedroom on which I had woken up.

It was 4.00 a.m. in the morning and still quite dark. In my

total ignorance of the situation, plus my muddled state of my mind, I immediately assumed it must have been an earthquake. I could be forgiven for this assumption, for up to that time I had never been near, or even had to face even the slightest of these natural earth occurrences.

The strong smell of dust mixed with a variety of other toxic ingredients permeated the atmosphere of my room causing me to violently choke.

After picking myself up from the floor I was surprised to notice that with the limited help of the back lighting provided by the street lamps, not one pane of glass appeared to be cracked in my front window, which overlooked the normally busy street. At this time of morning, all should have been quiet, it wasn't, certainly not today, for this was very different situation from normal and I could distinctly hear the sound of voices, which were in the near vicinity, plus the raucous blare emitted from a large number of fast approaching sirens.

Without further delay and still in semi-darkness I headed across the room, narrowly avoiding stubbing my toes on the dressing table, which was now on its side, with difficulty I negotiated around a couple of upturned chairs. Successfully I reached the window in an attempt to let some fresh air inside the bedroom, thus protecting my lungs from any further harm, I was certainly disappointed, for under its present condition the metal frame turned out to be solidly jammed and immovable.

Closely examining the window I easily realised the reason for the lack of broken glass, for it was not glass, but a strongly translucent plastic material that had replaced the original panes.

I then decided to find a second line of defence, for having read books on how to avoid injury during the Californian tremors; my attention had been drawn to examine the doorframe of my bedroom, this was to see if it was strong enough to bare the weight of the wall above, should it be necessary to give me shelter, I considered this would at least afford some temporary protection against any aftershock. On examination it appeared to be quite a strong and thankfully quite wide.

Of course this depended upon my pre-conceived idea that it have been an earthquake.

After thirty minutes, and without even the slightest of tremors taking place, I decided to dress fully and investigate what damage had been caused outside the building.

With some exertion I opened the flat door and stepped onto the staircase, surprisingly the small landing light was still working and I could see that the floor and steps had been coated with a thick covering of plaster from the ceiling.

I entered the street as the first glimmer of light announced the coming of dawn.

A large crowd of people was standing nearby; many dressed in their nightclothes, whilst a few individuals could be seen just draped in towels. The bulk of the citizens were less than six feet from the door from which I had exited and in the gloom, I could observe they were looking up at a huge hole in the brickwork in the flat next to mine, no natural phenomenon in this case but possibly a gas cooker. I then remembered there was no gas supply in this building, and my next thought chilled my bones as I realized what it was, for it had to have been, a man-made bomb.

The street soon completely filled with people spilling onto

the main highway and blocking the pathway of the emergency vehicles.

The cacophony of sound from their blaring claxons did the trick, as the crowd scattered and the frustrated drivers were able to pull up outside the house.

The red flashing lights reflected eerily against the white walls of the building as a dozen or so army and police vehicles drew up in the street outside.

Within a very short time, several smartly dressed officers had commenced to interview the tenants of our block. My turn for questioning never came, for within five minutes my eyes were drawn in amazement to a large black man, whom I could see was being roughly bundled into the back of a grubby 'black Maria' prison van, which lost no time in driving away from the scene.

Thankfully, I soon learned that nobody had been killed and although it was an extremely dangerous deed, it had been no more than a personal vendetta by the fellow, openly venting his feelings towards the increased rents from his white landlord, no doubt with the lack of fatalities the perpetrator would be spared the noose. Which at that time in the country's history was the common form of justice, and I must add, still is today.

My early days in Zimbabwe had been truly launched with fire and a wonderful show of Gods protecting powers; If I had only known the future then; I would have prepared myself for the start of countless episodes which I would have to face over the next thirty-five years or so.

CHAPTER 1

Christchurch Baptist Church

God's plan is definite and needs to be prayerfully sought and diligently adhered to even if we do not understand it.

A few months after marrying my wife I took on the position of running the heating department of Bournemouth Corporation which I so enjoyed and now, a few years on, I felt depressed that during the last few weeks I was told that my comfortable yet demanding job had come to an end. I was to be made redundant *(no redundancy pay in those days).*

Out of desperation I took up employment with the National Health Service at Christchurch Hospital. A few days later, in the hospital maintenance department workshop, whilst having my lunch break, I picked up one of the newspapers that was lying about, I remember it well, for it had been the *'The Daily Mirror'.*

I had taken up the position as hospital plumber and I hated going back to cleaning drains, changing washers and clearing sluices. Something I had not done since I was twenty-one, in fact working in a hospital reminded me of a tricky situation I had been involved in during an early stage in my plumbing apprenticeship. It was whilst I had been working on an extension to Wimborne Cottage Hospital in Dorset, my hometown.

It had been 10.00 a.m. and time for our morning break. Being the youngest person on the site I was automatically enlisted as the tea boy. A groundsman had told me that a water tap was installed in a small vegetable patch at the rear of the hospital; he also informed me that the gardeners had lit a fire, and I could use it to boil the kettle.

In those days, the hospital grew a lot of their own vegetables for the kitchen, probably after the fairly recent years of austerity and post war rationing.

The murky coloured water supply from the tap ran very slowly into the black soot-stained kettle, which was a great surprise to me, as our town's water supply was normally extremely clean and powerful.

Once the kettle was filled, I placed the pot on the glowing wood fire and waited for it to boil. After making the tea I called the other workmen, about ten in number, and we sat around the blazing wood fire on a long plank, the splinter free board had been placed on two piles of bricks.

With a benevolent grin on his face the foreman said how much he liked the taste of the tea, *"it tastes so different today, and in fact you can always make it now!"* Then almost as an afterthought he added, *"Where did you get the water from?"* I showed him the garden tap and watched his face in amazement, as instantaneously he turned a funny colour, and without delay declared, *"That was the septic tank test point."* (*We had no main drainage in Wimborne in those days*) Needless to say I was never asked to make the tea again, although I cannot remember anyone being sick. Unfortunately my work colleagues treated me with total contempt, and from then on and for the rest of the week I was sent to Coventry.

I am certain this episode had left me indelibly scarred, and as I remarked earlier, my work surroundings at the Hospital had re-kindled once again my dislike at being in my present environment.

The newspaper that I was reading held a number of interesting positions and one insertion motivated my mind in its direction. This advertisement was for an engineering job on 'Permutit', at that time a famous and very prolific English water-softening firm. They wanted to train service engineers to work on their products throughout the UK.

Lilian, and I with our two children Simon and Amanda were living in the historic town of Christchurch and like most people in the nineteen sixties (*and even today for a large number of the population*) we were struggling to pay the mortgage and bills.

This job looked very promising and offered a far better wage than I was now earning, hopefully no more arriving home from work with Lilian having to go out almost immediately to the local cinema, *'The Regent'* where she was employed working as a cashier during the evenings to help pay the mortgage.

It was on December 4th 1954 when I was 14 years of age, that I became a Christian. It was at a Youth for Christ meeting in the local Methodist church in Wimborne and the experience had taken place during a Billy Graham film (*Oil town USA*).

Although I had always attended the local Baptist church it was the first time I had recognized that I needed to give my heart to the Lord Jesus Christ and accept his death on the cross as a sacrifice for my sins. Since then I firmly believed that I had been led and directed to a future chosen by God.

On this particular day I felt that this was the right job to apply for, and without letting the grass grow under my feet, I had posted my letter of application within a few hours of reading the advert.

Several weeks passed without any response from the company, in fact I almost forgotten that I had sent my application, then, quite by surprise I received a letter inviting me to attend an interview at the 'Dolphin Hotel' Southampton.

This once famous venue had been an old coaching inn, not far from the well-known and very famous Southampton docks, I was quite familiar with the city, which until we got married in 1964 had been my wife's birthplace and home, this was not the only thing to take place in Southampton during that year, for the town became a city.

I have forgotten the details of the interview, but needless to say my future changed for the good from that day, as within two weeks I was offered the post of service engineer working from my home.

I attended a so-called course for training, which I have to say was far less informative than I could ever have expected.

Its content consisted mainly of service reports which involved lots of form filling; virtually no technical knowledge was given to me whatsoever, in fact not even a handbook that would enable me to repair their equipment.

Instead of the two-week training school that I had been promised, I was given a white van and sent out to attend breakdowns the very next day, covering the Greater London area.

My ignorance on my new venture was absolute; in fact, I hardly knew what the majority of water softeners even looked like. The excuse given to me, claimed that the local engineer's had been on leave!

This was long before the days of satellite navigation or talking phones, just street maps and trial and error; talk about a novice, yet somehow I bumbled my way through.

For quite a few years Lilian and I worshipped in Christchurch Baptist Church and there we experienced the hand of God visibly working, this included what I believe to have been a number of miracles. The following incident took place whilst I had been giving a demonstration in acid cleaning on an industrial, demineralised water treatment plant in the main boiler house of Yeovil District Hospital in Somerset.

I had explained the correct dosage of sulphuric acid to my audience and also the safety aspects during the procedure of cleaning the internal resins[1] of the machine. Quite unexpectedly a slight mist appeared to rise about me, similar to what we now see during many musical presentations on television. Slowly my legs became partly hidden from view.

---

[1] *The material within the unit that supplied the pure water required by*

Completely different to any stage show I had ever seen, for on this occasion I remember all too clearly the strong, pungent smell which caused the hairs in my nostrils to melt; within seconds I realized that this was the gas given off by the acid following its contact with the air I was inhaling. The source of the problem quickly became apparent, as I looked up at the acid storage floor above me; I noticed that a '*carboy*' had split and its deadly contents were gently spraying over me. Within seconds my shoes had been filled with the acid. No doubt caused by the deadly corrosive liquid as it ran down my trousers. Remarkably I felt no panic, but asked, *"Where is the water tap?"* The spontaneous reply I received from my audience. *"Not working"* (*no great 'health and safety' in those days*), so I put my foot in the nearest toilet and pulled the chain. Not much use, so a wheelchair that previously I had not noticed was utilized and with great speed I was pushed down a precipitous path beside the boiler house across a main road and into the emergency entrance to the hospital, *(The only fear for me was if they lost control of the chair on the steep hill).*

The doctor came to me instantly and after looking at my leg, which had turned black said these words, *"Mr Clarredge, I am sorry you are badly burned."*

I answered with the words: *"I am Ok."*

Very carefully she peeled off what she had conceived to be a mixture of jet black, badly burnt skin and clothes; once removed, the doctor had been amazed to see that my body hairs were untouched and it had certainly been God who protected me.

The next weekend I stood at the front of a packed church holding up the remnants of my trousers as a testimony to

God's protection. Positively from that moment I knew that He must have had something far greater planned for my life.

Lilian and I took over a small group of young people in our church and with pleasure and joy we both watched the group grow beyond all expectations joining in with local social events, yet more important than that, witnessing the power of God working under the anointed power of the Holy Spirit in their lives.

Our young people's group met in *'the upper room'* at Christchurch Baptist Church, and I remember one night witnessing that I should share a *'word of knowledge'* with the group, which I believe I had been given by The Holy Spirit. This would certainly show God working amongst them, and would increase my faith.

I must add that there was no outside advertisement of our meeting whatsoever. *"I believe that three people will come tonight and find Jesus Christ as their Saviour."*

I remember the incredulous look on the faces of the group. The meeting continued for at least half an hour, before I heard footsteps coming up the stairs, first one young man, then another and finally a blind man.

The presence of God was very real during that meeting, and within a few minutes of their arrival, tears started to roll down the faces of the first two men; and long before the meeting was over they had made a decision to give their lives to Christ.

Our evening together finished and one young person who is now a pastor challenged me, "*You said three?*"

I could not explain why only two out of the three came forward, that is until late in the evening when Chris the blind man phoned me and asked me to pray with him, during that conversation he too gave his life to the Lord.

Many acts of testimony came out of that group, even winning the Christmas carnival with a float depicting the Christian message; the judges' comments shook both Lil and I, *"How unusual for this time of the year."*

My new job was somewhat demanding, yet I can look back with great satisfaction and realise how much my life had changed, routine was gone and the many work challenges I daily experienced, both taught me and also pointed me in the direction that I now knew that God had chosen for me.

My five years of training as a plumber took place in the town of Poole in Dorset, my birthplace and had been a good discipline in my education, although at times I felt like running away I learnt a word which I have used countless times since '*stickability.*'

I had a heart attack when I was only thirty-seven-years-old, whilst working for Permutit, and thankfully through the faithful prayers of my wife and the young people at Christchurch Baptist Church I completely recovered. My company then asked if I would mind helping out in the regional office at Shepton Mallet in Somerset on a regular basis.

Whilst I had been off sick through my heart attack and during a period of British austerity when companies were forbidden to give salary rises, I received a type of *'round robin'* letter saying that if we were prepared to work overseas we could have a raise of sixpence an hour.

How I longed to work overseas yet even through this loophole in the law it certainly helped us financially. God provided in a very special way as I had developed a condition called peripheral neuropathy and had great difficulty in coordinating my hands and feet, this condition was as yet unknown to my employers, but made life extremely difficult for me, through being rather stubborn by nature, I still managed to carry out my daily physical work without losing any time for the company.

Permutit was expanding and losing their London based technical manager through retirement. To my utter amazement I received a letter suggesting that I should apply for the post of domestic technical advisor to the company, filling the vacancy created by a retiring employee, this involved attending an interview at our head office in Hounslow but with the proviso that I would have to live in London. (*The establishment had no idea of any health problems other than my coronary but I also knew that the new post would not involve physical work and until I was healed would release me from extra stress.*)

To my surprise I was the only person attending the interview and after less than five minutes my future manager had left me in the office with a telephone, and with the instruction to call my wife and ask if she was prepared to move to London.

Although not wishing to leave our home She agreed to me taking up the position. From that moment, our lives were once again to take on a brand-new direction.

I prayed with the deacons at the church and to my dismay the pastor said that through my health problems he felt that I should not accept the job, strange advice considering the church believed in prayer for the sick and some of us had even experienced magnificent healings, including a lady in Wimborne Dorset whom I had known since a child, called Marjorie Stevens who had been completely healed of Multiple Sclerosis.

As I have said, it was a great blessing that I would not be using my hands in this job.

I laid a fleece that if it was not Gods plan then I would not get the accommodation I required, so I set out for the next month trying to obtain somewhere to live within the Hounslow or Ealing areas of Greater London. I was totally unsuccessful even though I visited the local churches in the Brentford area seeking somewhere reasonable to reside.

I then began to question if it was God's plan, and asked myself if the Pastor had been correct? Should I now resign, somewhat embarrassing under the circumstances? To have to leave the job that I had grown to love, throwing away my new position within the company, which I had not even commenced?

Then a miracle took place; we had some elderly friends who had been nurses in the London area and had retired from the capital to Christchurch; Lilian and me regularly visited the two sisters.

The week prior to my supposed move to London I visited the sisters and was quickly ushered into their lounge. They had a visitor, an elderly lady staying with them who was slumped somewhat despondently in a chair. The poor woman had the saddest tear-stained face I have ever seen.

After a brief introduction I discovered her name was Winn, I shared my difficulties with the nurses and almost immediately in what I took to be a call of nature, the lady left the living room.

This gave the opportunity for me to be told of the reason behind Winn's profound grief. It was because her husband had died just a few weeks previous and she could not face going to her home in 'Ealing' alone.

After quite a long time Anne left the lounge and I assumed this was to check if Winn was Ok. In a short time they both returned to the room and I could not fail to notice a transformation on the woman's face; I am sure you have guessed it!

God had answered my prayer, and hers, no wonder I didn't find accommodation for she did not have to go home alone, I had my house for just a few pounds a week, added to this I would not have to sell our house in Christchurch, or have to take our children away from their school.

God proved to me that it was His will and He was in charge. For me it was a continuation of faith building in a huge and extremely practical way leading to a valuable training period for what was to come.

My new position was an eye opener to the human race, certainly following a catastrophic failure of a newly designed piece of equipment. Initially the job entailed pacifying the existing customers and replacing every faulty water softener. Once that work was completed I only visited specific patrons if they had problems. This involved certain well know film and TV stars that were a good advertisement for the company.

One humorous incident comes to mind; this was when I visited a previous *Dr Who*, from the BBC TV series who is no longer with us. It appeared that he had struggled to set up his time clock. With tongue in cheek, I commented that if he could drive a time machine surely he could set up a time clock. His explosive temperament took over instantly and articles near to where he was standing took to the air with dangerous rapidity, in fact it took his lovely wife at least five minutes to calm him down before he stomped off to his private study. I didn't see him again, (*except for TV appearances*). His wife apologized most profusely to me for his behaviour. Through this occurrence I quickly learnt to keep my humour in obeyance.

During my period of dealing with disgruntled customers I arranged to replace a newly designed machine in a Bishop's palace some 200 miles from home. The gentleman's manner was absolutely obnoxious on the telephone, and although I did not believe his softener was faulty, I arranged to meet an engineer on site with a plan to replace it. I had left Christchurch very early on the Monday morning and arrived about 10.00am with an identical machine in my car.

When I met the Bishop, his manner was distinctly icy and I felt like telling him of God's love, (*and quoting 1 Corinthians 13*) however I told the engineer to check the appliance whilst the Bishop stood over us breathing fire and brimstone, the machine showed a perfect reading.

Rather than be subject to further verbal abuse I told the engineer to change it; I opened the packing case holding the new machine, and to my absolute horror found it to be severely damaged. Quick thinking was vital and very quietly I told the engineer to give the impression we had swopped it over, whilst I found a way of diverting the Bishop's gaze.

"Sir, I have had a long journey and would like to use your toilet, may I?"

The man pointed to what appeared to be a brick-built

structure some distance away, in fact at the end of his very large garden, informing me *"it's there."*

With quick thinking I responded, *"Sorry sir I don't see it."*

His anger showed and he virtually frog marched me some 300 yards or so until we came to the gardeners *'rest room,'* a cold, badly smelling place filled with aroma's from an assortment of fertilisers.

I loitered inside the building for about five minutes and hoped the Bishop would still be there; thankfully, the fuming cleric was still outside waiting impatiently.

We then walked back to my engineer; I guess the whole process took less than ten minutes. The smiling face of the engineer greeted us as he said without lying, *"all done and the other machine is in my van"*. He failed to say which softener!

The bishop looked incredulous as he stated, *"Impossible, if this doesn't work then I will have your guts for garters."*

Certainly not the language I would have expected from any clergyman; let alone a Bishop, Little more was said and without any thanks from the priest, or even a cup of coffee offered, I returned to London.

Needless to say within two weeks he had phoned my office to say he had been correct from the beginning, as the 'new' machine was perfect!!

Having maintained water treatment equipment within the fast-growing area of Renal Dialysis during my days as a service engineer it was decided by my managers that I should be professionally trained in the specialised field of water used for blood cleaning as a technician. I undertook my tuition first at Liverpool Royal Infirmary and later at Cardiff Royal Infirmary.

I then took a new role in re-designing specific equipment for use on dialysis machines, Spending time testing these at the NHS Hallamshire laboratories situated within the University of Sheffield.

Once technically qualified, my title changed to that of Medical Advisor to the company dealing primarily with renal dialysis. If only I had known then, the importance for my future in Africa initially depended on my knowledge within the field of dialysis.

God's plan was still evident for after a short period of time my peripheral neuropathy completely disappeared; then sadly Winn went to be with the Lord, and her relatives gave me a week's notice to leave the house. Once again, God's hand intervened, for within a few hours they had discovered there was no will and asked me to live in the house rent free until probate was completed. I would have been homeless as far as the company was concerned.

Through God's grace not only had my address remained the same, but also at the end of six months I received temporary accommodation supplied by one of her friends.

It was not long after this, in fact I recollect almost immediately, that I learnt that there was to be a re-organization and I was likely to face a job change. I was informed of this by telephone whilst I was working at Leeds Royal Infirmary *(Jimmy's from the current ITV. television programme of that period)*, despondency instantly set in.

Driving home on the motorway I stopped at the Watford gap services, thankfully it was particularly good weather and feeling rather unsociable due to my news. I sat outside the building on a long wooden picnic table.

Facing me was another fellow whose whole appearance gave me the impression that he too was deeply concerned about something. We got into conversation and I explained my present concerns over my employment, his eyes appeared to bulge from his forehead as he told me his problem. He worked for Culligan a huge American company whose UK base was situated in High Wycombe; he had a problem for, through medical reasons, they had recently lost their '*dialysis medical advisor*' from a newly formed renal department.

The very next day I attended an interview in High Wycombe and was invited by the managing director to join the company as soon as I could.

Within three days I had moved companies and have to say that this was the start of my work overseas, and my eventual work in the continent of Africa.

CHAPTER 2

Air Zimbabwe

The year was 1983 and without even realizing it, the time since joining the company had passed like wildfire, in fact by now we were well into the month of June, meaning we were halfway through the year already.

I had just finished a short stint working in Belgium at our Brussels office, and was glad to return home, not only to be with my family, but also to catch up on a backlog of work that had piled up whilst I had been away.

It was a Monday 21st June and without knowing it then, that particular date would become indelibly etched in my mind.

I left home at 5.30 in the morning to cover the one hundred- and six-mile drive that stretched between my home in Christchurch, Dorset and my office in High Wycombe, Buckinghamshire; thankfully, there were no holdups on the road, and the journey proved to be completely uneventful and trouble free.

At least the light traffic had allowed me to arrive quite early in the morning, and I felt completely at ease knowing that I would be able to carry out a full day's work at Culligan's UK base.

As I walked into the main office an extremely frustrated company secretary greeted me. I remember being quite surprised that he was there, for it was at least two hours earlier than his usual time of arrival.

Entering the office I noticed that in his hand he held a very long sheet of paper, which, as far as I could make out was a fax.

He hardly gave me time to take my coat off before accosting me. Charles (*For that was his name*) achieved this by pushing the communication to the front of my face, with the words, "*Look at this.*"

The headline instruction from the USA read quite simply; '*send Alan Clarredge to Harare in July for the trade fair*' and then continued with what at first glance appeared to be a list of instructions followed by the details for my visit.

Without delay he stated his dilemma, *"where on earth is Harare?"* As far as I was concerned his problem had been quite logical, especially at that particular era of world history. I considered the speed at which new countries were emerging through the process of independence, and understood just a little of the confusion that he felt.

No Internet or search engines were available in those days; in fact, the only computer I had used, held an old version of *Britannica*, and the changes of the names in so many of the

African countries during the past few years had been sufficient to make my version of the encyclopaedia geographically redundant.

He once again emphasized his quandary, *"Whom do I book the flight with and where is Harare?"*

At least he knew from the fax he had received that it was Africa, but as everybody who has been taught geography in school would know, the size of Africa was absolutely colossal, Harare could have been anywhere between Egypt and South Africa for all we knew?

I felt excitement rising from the pit of my stomach as I remembered something from my childhood. It was the year 1949 when I was only nine years of age; we had a missionary on furlough from the Belgium Congo visiting our church. He was a good speaker and I remember him telling us a number of exciting stories from the Congo; one of which vividly described an incident when he and his fellow workers were in absolute danger from a band of terrorists, and how the bandits had run away when they were accosted by a heavenly band of angels that were in the guise of soldiers, no human forces were involved. I was agog, accepting every word and believing as I do up to this day, that they had survived and managed to achieve great results in that country because of the Almighty Power of God that had been with them.

My Sunday school teachers name was Miss Tilly and after this visit she had provided us with a sticker books containing many blank spaces, these had to be filled weekly with picture stamps. The stamps were one old penny each in aid of the Baptist Missionary Society, which after a few weeks when the brochure was full showed a completed picture of a colourful native village, filled with brightly clothed children playing outside their roundel-thatched house. After looking at these pictures and remembering the story we had so recently been told, I had been fired up and I clearly remember telling Miss Tilly that one day I hoped to be a missionary in what had been referred to in the nineteen forties, as the Dark Continent.

Some 34-years had passed since that time; yet somewhere deep inside my head, that spark was still there, and gave me once again the desire to work in Africa.

This would be my first trip to the continent of Africa and I trusted it would be in Gods will and purpose for me to serve Him in some way there in the future, if only I had known how much at that time.

It took a long time to discover that Harare had previously been called Salisbury, which was an English Cathedral City in Wiltshire not far from where we now live, and the college where my theological training to become a minister in the URC happened to take place, of course my ordination took place a little later in my life.

The country was Zimbabwe and at that time had its own airline called *Air Zimbabwe* which flew directly from Gatwick Airport; south of London; to the capital city Harare.

Philip the company accountant was a kind man and in the absence of the MD said, "*I'm getting you into business class it's a long journey.*"

I spent the next two weeks deep in preparation for the trip, reading up all the information I could get from my *Britannica.* Admittedly the data was somewhat out of date since independence. Even so, there was still a great deal of relevant information about the country, as I have said from my prologue, the state had previously been called Southern Rhodesia, and I got the best help I could in learning of its cultural background.

I knew I would have to pack a lot of knowledge into my brain before going, which was quite good for me. Due to a pre-arranged holiday I was only able to stay in Zimbabwe for ten days, before returning home.

Our family holiday had been booked long before this visit to Harare, so I knew planning for my next few weeks could only be described, as quite daunting.

Once I had returned home from Zimbabwe, it would only be three days before we had to face a long drive down to Yugoslavia on our packaged holiday. This involved lots of stops both going and then returning home, looking at the maps supplied by our travel agent, I could see that it would be quite a complicated journey, however hopefully not as complex or frustrating as my Zimbabwean trip would be.

My instruction had been quite clear, stating that on my arrival a certain Mr Hawkins who had arranged my board would take me to my accommodation in the Harare Club, he would meet me at 6.30 a.m. at the airport.

It was a good and fairly comfortable night flight on a Boeing 707 and I even spent a short time in the cockpit with the two pilots and their engineer, before settling back in my wide leather chair.

I was served a very good meal; far superior to the meals served these days, and after eating a quite delicious meal; compared to modern catering, I watched an extremely blurred film on the two-foot screen that hung from the roof of the cabin, until I fell asleep.

My rest didn't last long, probably because I was far too excited and longed to arrive at my destination, so a number of short catnaps had to do.

However when morning eventually came my lack of sleep had little effect on me, no doubt the adrenalin produced in my bloodstream combined with the excitement of my arrival at the beautiful white painted colonial airport carried me through.

My problems started instantly as I quickly filled out the entry document. The immigration officer gave me a strange look as he said, *"I crossed out the part you ticked which stated you had been serving a prison sentence in the UK. You look too honest for me!"* We both laughed and I passed through to the baggage reclaim; no hold up there and I emerged into the spacious reception area of the large airport.

I looked at a large number of boards with names written upon them, mine was not there, in fact after walking up and down in front of the couriers it did not take me long to discover that nobody had turned to meet my flight.

I have to admit I was left in a deep quandary, as to what I should do. For after hanging about for at least an hour in a now deserted entrance hall I had to make a decision on what to do?

I decided to question each cabbie that remained in the fairly long line of taxis waiting outside the airport entrance, asking each in turn if they knew of *'the Harare club'*?

Only one '*RIXI*' cab driver said he did, and some twenty minutes later after passing at least a hundred tall poles with banners portraying Mr Mugabe's face on the top of them, we reached the *'Harare Cricket Club'*. After a fierce and totally unnecessary *(I guessed)* argument between my driver and the cricket club steward, I was given the correct address of the club. (*The dispute was never actually explained to me*).

Eventually I arrived at the correct location in Third Street, stopping in the beautiful African Unity Square outside the impressive Parliament building. The trees and shrubs were in full bloom and I managed to take a photograph. This was too my cost, as I was instantly accosted by the military police, as unbeknown to me I had also photographed an ambulance parked nearby; outside the Parliament building in case anything happened to the Prime Minister Robert Mugabe. I was told later that his conveyance was always there whenever Parliament was in session and he was present.

After a stern lecture, my film was removed from the camera and I was ordered to move along. This all took place just a few metres from the correct, Harare Club.

My accommodation was within a modern high-rise building with a few waterless fountains outside its entrance.

Once inside, my whole perspective changed for the modern exterior had been replaced by traditional dark wood panels, these spoke to me of a different era, added to this, the excessive smell of Lavender polish which reminded me of what I had read about in my childhood in the magazines of the day, such as The Tatler the *London Illustrated News*; and comically *Punch* which had many pictures of the men's clubs situated in the Pall Mall area of London.

The almost overpowering smell of floor polish reminded me of the wooden floors in my old school from childhood.

Beside my bed on an old, yet highly polished oak table

stood a shiny brass bell, evidently for me to use, should I need to call the bellboy. He was seated at the end of a long corridor. The smoky lounge and dining room had a bad effect on my breathing, and within a short space of time, I was extremely glad to escape into the fresh air of the outside pavement.

My sponsor arrived with no explanation or apology for not picking me up, and immediately showed his only interest was that being the purchase of my English pounds; I soon learned that this was the 'normal' practice during this period of the country's history, although it was highly illegal if caught doing it, In fact this was the only way that people could get hold of British pounds, should they want to leave the country, (*unless they had a wealthy overseas family to foot the bill)* this means of laundering money was never explained to me by my ex-Rhodesian managing director in the UK.

Once the exchange had been completed he gave me the address of my Zimbabwe sponsors, whose premises happened to be less than ten minutes away from my accommodation.

It was a lovely morning and I found it extremely interesting to walk down through the crowded street to the area in which the office was situated.

It was a small, brown corrugated building with a high roof, not unlike the shape of a typical wooden chapel found in countless English towns and villages.

Culligan was a part of Avis car hire, which was conveniently, situated just a couple of hundred metres from my temporary workplace. Expected by the staff I immediately received a car, which proved to be absolutely essential in my programme.

Passmore the son of an employee within my sponsors

company joined me, and together we made our way to the Showground.

My stand was huge, with four trestle tables and bereft of anything but two chairs that looked as though they had seen better days.

Although promised, my company in the UK had failed to send me any demonstration water treatment equipment plants, to place on the stand, all I had were a dozen or so leaflets describing our products.

In those days, the 'Harare Show' was very prolific, and only carried stands that were booked, and well presented by the best companies in Zimbabwe.

The goods that were offered were a demonstration of their hope in a new country. Very professionally I must add, not only local businesses but also goods from neighbouring countries such as South Africa, Malawi and Botswana, although I did notice a contingency from much further north, in fact on the Equator, Kenya. We were the only British company represented.

Mainly the products on show were agricultural and our equipment would have been good for the rural areas and industry.

I knew I had a hard task ahead and along with Passmore we visited a number of travel agents with the endeavour to obtain as many '*water related*' posters as possible. Air Zimbabwe provided me with pictures of lake Kariba on the Zambezi, also many shots of Victoria Falls. Another local agent provided me with several pictures of Lake McIlwaine a huge reservoir serving Harare and district named in memory of Sir Robert McIlwaine, a former judge of the High Court and founder of Southern Rhodesia's soil and water conservation movement (*The reservoir is now called Lake Chivero*).

I am no artist but I drew the company logo on some A1 posters along with a brief description of our products geared to my present environment, once completed I have to admit, that far from perfect, at least the stand had taken on a much more local and personable effect.

The opening day came, and I had been told that I would have two special visitors at 2.00 p.m. in the afternoon the Prime Minister of that time Robert Mugabe, and with him President Jawaharlal Nehru.

Some farmers conversed with me in the morning, then in preparation for my important visitors I decided to have an early lunch leaving Passmore to man the stand, until I returned at 12.30.

2.00 p.m. plus an extra hour passed by and I felt frustrated that my red-carpet guests had failed to arrive, it was only after I had moaned to my young colleague that he informed me the dignitaries had visited the stand two hours early at 12.00 mid-day. *"They liked the stand boss,"* had been his words; I failed to inform my UK Company of this fact and reported back that night to my office explaining that it might be good for me to visit some needy areas whereby I may be able to help.

It was agreed that Passmore should man the stand whilst I visited a number of these areas.

Reginald Ghona, Passmore's father joined me and together we made the return trip to Bulawayo about 400 kilometres each way (*Approx. 250 miles*).

We left Harare at about 4.30 in the morning and we drove to this the second largest City in Zimbabwe, it was in

Matabeleland (*The south of the country*) and there was a noticeable coolness towards my companion when we arrived,

The reason being he was Shona, and under Robert Mugabe there had been a wholesale slaughter of the Ndebele races prior to independence.

My heart was going out to the people of the rural areas, not knowing the many years, even up to this day that I should be working in Matabeleland.

I visited not only the water works but also Mpilo Hospital, which was situated, on the outskirts of the city.

At that time there were less difficulties than today but still shortages and some of the rural districts needed help. Every stop whet my appetite to help those good people.

What I did not realise was, that God had a much bigger plan than I was seeing before my eyes. His plan at that time was one of preparations for what was to come, including my involvement with a fully-fledged civil war not too far from Zimbabwe in Mozambique.

As I boarded the plane for home I glanced up to the long white veranda to see Ghona's larger than life family members standing there waving their hands in my direction. How many were there I could only guess but at least twenty of them, perhaps even more.

For me leaving Zimbabwe was sad but something told me I would soon be coming back soon.

CHAPTER 3

Within three weeks of my return from Yugoslavia and following a number of feasibility studies having taken place. It was decided I should return to Zimbabwe. This time for a month to enable me to visit several areas of this vast country and meet a number of water board officers. During which I learned of the shortages, learnt of the problems and began to be successfully Africanised by the local population.

I found a church to attend, this was situated in the district of Eastlea within the boundaries of Harare, it was part of the Zimbabwe Assemblies of God under the pastoral leadership of John Baker. I was thrilled to start the process of bonding with John and the church, in fact I was very blessed in a different way, for arriving in the locality I was under the misapprehension that once there, I could easily contact my wife using a public telephone, unfortunately from the first day I learnt that working phone boxes did not exist and it was through the auspices of a young couple within the church that I was allowed the use of their phone and make an expensive call to tell Lil I had arrived safely.

One incident, (*not humorous at the time*) which still remains in my mind, was a trip to the mighty Kariba dam. The African company that I had been sent to work with decided I should meet the officials of this large town to see if we could become involved in a very large project of water purification.

The details laid out for their project were very precise and must have cost a small fortune to prepare, there were so many noughts on the figures regarding the work required that I could never really grasp its true value, my job was to check the quote provided to them by the Italian section of our company against the actual work required.

Preparations completed and the quote safely stored in the boot of our car I picked up Reginald and after dropping my colleagues children at school we set off for Kariba some 174 miles to the west of Harare.

We had barely covered 50 miles after leaving the city on the long journey before we encountered our first problem! It came when I had to fill up the car with petrol, and commenced when Reginald Ghona told me that he had spent the money we had been allocated by the company for our trip, the trouble was his boss had personally given it to him!! On reflection I would have thought that the boss would have had more sense than trust him with the money. "*I had to pay school fees for my children,*" had been his excuse. I soon learnt that this was a typical thing to happen in Zimbabwe. *"You must have money boss?"* I knew I had enough money to get us to Kariba and perhaps 40 or 50 miles for our return journey, but certainly no more!!

We continued the journey to Kariba under the promise given to me by Reginald, that on our arrival he had relatives who would give him the money that he had 'borrowed' from me. I very quickly learnt on our arrival in the city that these so-called called *'relatives'* were only his acquaintances and did not even enough money to keep themselves, let alone give cash to this so-called thieving nephew.

My next problem occurred quite suddenly, and was totally unexpected; leaving me utterly stunned. I was seated at a long table alongside a number of civic dignitaries, I have to say that I felt the members the town council should have forgiven me a little more graciously than they did over the occurrence, certainly as it was a total accident. Sorry I go too fast.

On my arrival at Kariba, the town clerk had presented me with a set of complicated and beautifully drawn plans for the new water purification works, *"These are for your examination and comments, take care of them,"* had been his comments. I have to admit on examination of the drawings, I felt extremely inadequate for it was a much larger project than I had ever seen or worked on before, and left me in a quandary as to my so called 'expertise' for the work. Nervousness at the implications should I make a mistake, caused salty perspiration to run down my forehead like a small river, stinging my eyes as I looked at the drawings, *(although looking back with hindsight it could well have been the 40° temperature that made me sweat).*

As I have just said it was very hot and there was very little breeze from the vast lake stretching for hundreds of Kilometres behind the dam. We were sitting in the town hall garden as I carefully scrutinised the only set of plans they possessed; our table had been placed under the shade of several small trees. Without warning, a rather large and extremely aggressive looking baboon ran past us, as he did, he grasped hold of the plans which were on the table before me and made off with them at the speed of an express train!!

"That will be the last we shall ever see those plans, you idiot." (added to this was a large variety of unwritten expletives). Certainly, I was left in no doubt the anger felt by the town clerk; dismay written across his face; my embarrassment was absolute, and after an apologetic excuse, we quickly left the town with his verbal abuse still ringing in my ears.

As we drove through the area I half expected to see a large number of monkeys with paper hats on their heads, made out of the plans. We didn't, and some 40 miles away the petrol gauge reached the red line, as somewhat fearfully I realised we were still some 130 miles from Harare.

It was at that point my colleague used his ingenuity, and stopping at every bus stop we picked up passengers and I embarrassingly collected their fares, and filling the car at every town we drove through. When we eventually arrived home Ghona turned to me and said, *"I made a profit today boss."*

Like Queen Victoria of old I was not amused. The very next day He was duly sacked by his boss on my recommendation and swore to get his own back on me, at a later date. How? You may well ask. But I will explain later in my story.

It was time to return to England for a short period of time to enable me to price up a number of smaller contracts, not much chance of that for almost immediately I was sent abroad once again.

*

To run a church in the UK at that time would have been impossible even though I had been pastoring a small mission hall at Ringwood in the New Forest. God knew the timing, for a month before leaving the UK we were told that the building we had been using was to be sold, and I spent the next few weeks with Lilian helping to move our young congregation to several other churches of their choice within the area.

God's timing is always perfect, and once the church was sorted out I was off to Budapest (*Still under communist control*) for a renal conference and it was during this conference that my future changed yet again.

I met a man from Zimbabwe his name was Obadiah Moyo *(in 2019 he became the Minister of Health for Zimbabwe)* and he told me that he needed me to be in Zimbabwe to oversee a venture that was to be financed by a top official of that country.

No argument within the company for they saw it as a good business venture, so yet once again, I ended up back in that beautiful African country.

After three months of preparation work I gave a quotation for the equipment required to set up five kidney units in different parts of the country including one for the Prime Ministers house for his wife's personal dialysis programme *(The special venture)* and after the submission I as forced to wait with bated breath for confirmation as to whether they wished me to supply the materials and install the units.

Still in Zimbabwe and quite unexpectedly, I had an urgent summons back to the UK, it sounded quite serious and I wondered what hot water I had got myself into? On my arrival in Gatwick at 6:30 a.m., I drove straight to the Culligan headquarters in High Wycombe and there I was told my department was to close down, and I was surplus to requirements.

I was shaken, £200 severance payment, no more Zimbabwe, nothing achieved, was this to be the end of my African dream I asked myself?

No certainly not, for within seven days I received a cheque made out to me personally for the purchase of equipment to supply pure water for six new kidney units stretching from Mutare in the Eastern highlands down to Bulawayo; including State House for Sally Mugabe's personal unit.

The Zimbabwean heath authority paid for my air ticket, and I was back in Harare in a short period of time awaiting the parts that I ordered to be delivered, thankfully I had paid for the equipment prior to its arrival.

I was not allowed to work, and would receive no wages until work commenced, but feeling secure that the finance for the equipment had been paid and the mark up would keep my family in the UK. I knew that sometime in the near future, I would receive a wage from the health service, unfortunately it was to be in Zimbabwe dollars, and the most I could send home would be £64.00 per month.

Strangely I felt totally confident at that time, living and working in a country that was becoming so dear to my heart.

Mr Moyo had sponsored my residency and I received official notification that I could receive a salary, once my residency came through, as long as I was working for the Health Service.

My next job was to find somewhere to live, away from the Bronte Hotel, which the government had paid for until I received my work permit.

Searching for accommodation was difficult, and I certainly needed somewhere to rent for my family and myself, especially during the school holidays, when they joined me in Harare.

I do well remember one humorous event that took place. The name on the real estate advertisement read *'Alan J. Clarridge'* Just one letter different from my own name I telephoned, and the conversation went like this. *"I would like a flat, please."*

"What is your name?"

"Alan Clarredge, yes it's Alan Clarridge" I replied.

"No, I am Alan Clarredge," after a few minutes of trying to persuade Alan who I was, I heard the phone being handed over to someone else in his office, and an older sounding voice said *"hello Son"* there followed a long discussion to prove we were not related. It ended with the information that no suitable flats were available.

Initially I had stayed in a number of cheap hotels and as my prologue describes even an unfortunate house sit.

My temporary residency came through, and I found it necessary to contact a local company that had been recommended to me, primarily to see if they would like the contract to construct the huge Fibreglass water tanks that were required for the hospitals. They jumped at the idea and the MD Patricia made great promises to me; *"There will be great benefits for both of us, you shall have the use of an office and we will find you accommodation and transport" (she failed to mention at that time, my residency permit would allow me to import two cars which they would pay for back in the UK and could freely bring into the country without paying any import duty; in exchange for this they gave me a low rent apartment and an ancient, yellow Ford Anglia car)*, the flat was situated in Avondale on the outskirts of the city; I soon gave the car a personal name; 'the yellow peril', for it spent more time in the garage than on the road, in fact it was more *'holy than righteous'* judging by the huge number of holes in its bodywork.

I still had sufficient conviction to trust the reason behind all that was taking place in my life, drawing the conclusion that it was to prepare me for a work prepared by God, in fact it was, far greater than I could ever have imagined.

CHAPTER 4

Puzey House

Within a short period of time I had moved into a totally new venue, and one which I was able to comfortably work from, it was situated in one of the oldest buildings in Harare called 'Puzey House' which was situated on Manica Road, being the old colonial name for the street in the British era. It has now been renamed Robert Mugabe Road.

This company as promised had arranged for the manufacture of the five huge water tanks required, which through sheer size, were required to be constructed locally; this for me was a great advantage because I did not have to purchase them overseas, with all the problems of shipment.

As I said under our agreement the company provided me with a nice, reasonably priced apartment at Avondale, which turned out to be a beautiful part of greater Harare.

I could now legally draw a wage from the 'Zimbabwe Kidney Fund' and knew this would cover not only my bills in running the apartment but would be sufficient to pay the wages of a '*housemaid*' to carry out my daily chores which included such items as washing, ironing plus polishing the beautiful wood floors. The local population of workers continuously changed as they travelled between the city and their families.

Most of their relatives still lived in the rural areas so it meant a constant variance of staff, most of these were very good. The last of these was Joice, whom I am still in touch with and support both her and her family through my church *(Joice was related to the late President Mugabe, although she had never met him personally).*

I did all the cooking myself, mainly steak, and to avoid boredom in my diet, I used a number of different sauces, which I was able to obtain locally from a small supermarket. My purchases also included a wide variety of herbs, which I utilized in my catering. Steak being the cheapest meat obtainable was economically sensible, certainly as I was now living on Zimbabwean wages. *(George the manager of the local supermarket had become a friend and kept many items under the shelves of the shop during the extended periods of shortages.)* After eating each evening, I gave food to my staff and this meant I did not have to wash up!!

The flat was wonderful and allowed Lil and the children who were now teenagers to join me during the school holidays. Each morning, excepting Sundays, my housegirl used to sit outside the front door and wait patiently for me to leave for work. Although I must admit, and I don't blame her, my wife did not appreciate the cleaner coming in at 6:30 a.m. and never got used to the idea of being a lady of leisure. Frightened of losing her job the maid not only washed dirty clothes but the clean ones as well!!

After fellowshipping in a number of good churches I eventually felt led to join a church in Hatfield on the outskirts of the city and very near to the airport, it was a small, *'Assemblies of God'* church. After a short time Philip Chigome joined the church as the Pastor and we became great friends working together as joint Pastors for the members of the fellowship. On most Sundays 'the yellow peril' let me down, and I had to walk the five miles to church.

This meant that I had to leave the flat at 7 a.m. in the morning, no hardship for me as I am an early riser. This enabled me to reach Hatfield for the 10.30 a.m. service, I have always hated being late for anything, especially for church on the Lord's day.

I found the walk to be inspiring and it was an added blessing for me to meet the friendly local people on the road and share about the Lord Jesus.

Eventually I received my AOG credentials and had the authority from the denomination to officially become a pastor and joint overseer for Hatfield. This was not only with Philip's blessing, but also followed a sincere and powerful request from the congregation, it also helped me considerably in the fact that I received a small stipend.

We had many happy times together and I well remember early one December when we celebrated a Christmas carol service, (this was *due to the fact that I was returning to the UK until*

January) it was agreed that I played the ancient piano for our carol service. Playing was not my favourite pastime, but I agreed, and alongside the young peoples' choir, and the worshippers joyful singing we raised the roof in a typical African style.

I followed the programme rigidly, or so I thought, for I came to the end of the carols sheet, and discovered they still had one hymn before they finished? Nobody noticed, or perhaps they were too polite to tell me.

It was a lovely church to belong to whilst I was there, and as the only white man I was made to be totally part of the fellowship, in fact even up to this day, being in touch with Philip and the church, especially when I am in Harare.

My next test of faith came when the equipment I had paid for, failed to arrive from the UK. I had spent a large proportion of the National Kidney Funds money, including a number of generous donations from Mr Mugabe, this whole situation left me feeling extremely uneasy.

For nearly three months I sent faxes from my Zimbabwe office. Each time I was told that it would be here tomorrow, tomorrow never seemed to come.

That was until one fateful day a message came through to me, it sent a cold shiver down my spine, for I was told that there had been an accident with Keune Nagels (*The shippers*) lorry on its way to the docks in England and every item I had purchased had been destroyed in the fire.

My daughter and Geoff my accountant in England chased the company to see if they had insured it, but Culligan told them that it was my responsibility!!

The cost would be in access of £38,000, at that time it

would have meant selling our house in the UK.

What could I do? But Pray!! The best thing for any believer to do, it was not only my prayers but also those of the United Reformed Church, which we attended at Throop in Bournemouth, and my church at Hatfield, my, how they prayed.

Lilian happened to be with me in Zimbabwe at this time, and naturally was as concerned as me.

Strangely until this time I had not been pressurized over the delivery time, yet the very next day Mr Moyo chased me, and asked when the machines and the rest of the equipment would arrive? Fear gripped me, and I failed to disclose my knowledge of the missing shipment, instead fobbing him off with a "*hopefully not long*". I was having visions of ending up in Chicarubi (*the worst Prison in Zimbabwe or so I had been told*). I did the only thing I could, I re-ordered the equipment arranging for it to be sent by air, the quickest means possible, thankfully for me Culligan didn't ask for payment upfront.

Lillian can vouch for the next stage that took place. For a further week or so this huge concern hung over me like a black cloud. The company continued to insist that I was responsible for the insurance.

Then one Sunday morning, I can indelibly remember the time, it was 3 a.m., and I had been lying fully awake in bed.

I felt strangely compelled to go into my home office, this was our spare bedroom, inside I had utilised the small wardrobe and filled the shelves with my papers, there were nine shelves, each was jam packed with documents. I had searched through the mixture of quotes and drawings numerous times in the hope of finding something that would release me from the responsibility of payment.

I pulled out a small pile of 'papers from the centre of the stack, and I must stress again, **these papers I had examined on numerous occasions**. When quite miraculously I found the original quote containing the words to say the contract was FOB. *(Free on board)*, and of course with all the equipment having been destroyed before the ship had been loaded in the UK I knew I was no longer responsible! Within a week a complete duplication of my previous shipment had arrived in Harare!

Peace of mind at last, and I knew another faith building exercise had been accomplished. All through this testing time my faith was growing, not only through this individual occasion but also on numerous minor occurrences including the revenge of Mr Ghona.

This took place when I was returning to the UK for a short break, all was going well, Lillian and myself had reached the airport and passed through the customs control. A guard sat on a high wooden desk in the centre of the corridor. Large screens had been placed through the middle of the passage ahead of me, which led to the departure lounge, and the uniformed officer directed the passengers heading to the terminal through two barriers, alternatively separating them, the first to the left and the second to the right and so on.

Lil was directed to the right-hand passage, whereby I was directed to the left.

As I passed a stern face customs officer, a carefully concealed door on my side opened quite silently and a hand came to rest my shoulder pushing me through the opening and into a well-lit office. The door instantly closed behind me. The white official was seated at a small desk and appeared to be perusing an extremely large folder. I clearly saw my name on the top, and asked myself how, in so short a period of time how could they have accumulated such a large dossier of my details, I must say it was quite worrying? Immediately he started to throw questions at me, some relevant, most not. Non-were racial but something about his manner of questioning made be deeply suspicious!

It must have been discernment on my part, as the ex-employee of my local company came to my mind, for at that moment I heard the interrogation officer utter the phrase *'living off immoral earnings'* I knew it could only happen through the lying tongue of Reginald.

He agreed that this was my accuser, and I immediately explained the reason behind his dismissal, causing my inquisitor to let out a loud peal of laughter, a phone call was immediately made and I was informed that it was to an extremely high official. Within two minutes and with the fellow still chuckling with great amusement, I was in the terminal building alongside my wife, who had not even realized the tricky situation I had been in.

One opportunity came my way when the pastor of another local church whom I knew very well invited me, to give a Christian *'thought for the day'* on the national radio station, ZBC. He gave me no warning, and only phoned me the night prior to the broadcast. He said he would like me to do the morning thought: it was Independence Day 1987 He continued by explaining it was a special day and felt it would be good for a white man to give a word of Christian encouragement. I felt very inadequate on the situation, yet God gave me the words as he always does and I had the opportunity as a European to congratulate them and give the gospel vocally in this new, at that time, very vibrant country.

I remember my Words of the Day as I addressed the Prime Minister Robert Gabriel Mugabe prior to him becoming President, on air I said that, *"This nation's future could be independent of England, but not of God."*

I was not arrested or criticised in this so-called communist country, but instead, given many opportunities to broadcast and talk of water, linking it with a spiritual application on numerous occasions.

In fact I even stood in for a disc jockey and took the Zimbabwe version of Top of the Pops, although it was in the 1980s, I was extremely thankful that their songs as they were still in the genre of the British pops of the 50s and 60s.

To give the gospel in Zimbabwe was not illegal even though it is a so-called communist country, in fact it could be said to be encouraged, and not yet contaminated with a lot of the scepticism and unbelief found in the west.

Through this, a strong Christian influence was provided both on radio and television in Zimbabwe; which proved invaluable to my future work in Mozambique.

My work in the various hospitals progressed and very slowly over many months I achieved the work of setting up the Kidney dialysis units starting in Harare.

It had its interesting moments plus its humorous ones, one particular incident took place whilst working in the Central Hospital, Harare, every lunchtime we would stop for our meal and a long form was positioned in the centre of the room, this seated about six of us. In front of this bench we put several small tables, on these was placed a number of sweet baked potatoes filled with minced avocado pears, and a mixture of lime juice, they were absolutely delicious and admitting for the first time it prejudiced my position in making this hospital my favourite for a short period of time.

The matron was an extremely large lady who wore flowing robes, and reminded me of the old black characters who always played the part of a lovely 'Mama' in the old American films, such as *Gone with the wind.*

On this occasion we were in the midst of a huge thunderstorm and the wide windows of the ward shook with the loud claps of thunder; combined with a dazzling reflection cast from the simultaneous sheets of lightning. The most nervous of our group was the matron, who placed her hands over her eyes, at every bright streak, *(belatedly I have to admit).*

We were all seated down ready to eat, when there was a particularly bright sheet of lightning, followed in less than a second by a thunderclap louder than any I had ever heard. Instantaneously we all jumped to our feet. Matron was a bit slower than the five of us, and her unqualified weight on the end of the long bench to which she was still adhered, caused it to spring high in the air, tipping the poor woman off quite suddenly, in fact all we could see was her white frilly dress sliding across the ward floor at a rate of knots that a speedboat would have difficulties in keeping up with.

She had a good sense of humour and for years after this occurrence she talked about it whenever I visited their hospital.

I had discovered that the thunderstorms in Zimbabwe were extremely dangerous, especially for those that lived in the bush.

There was little protection against the storms as many of the villagers would crowd into the larger of the grass roofed huts, only to be killed, as the bolt of lightning entered the roundel and encircled the walls before escaping the room.

In the early nineties, thick copper cables were distributed to many of the villages to be used in the form of lightning conductors. When fitted, hopefully this would cut the death toll *(I was always a little suspicious, of the motives, because Mr Mugabe got his best support in the elections from the rural people).*

Every day the list of fatalities grew, and I well remember reading in the national newspaper that the death toll from lighting strikes for that month was nearly 900 people.

A lot of my time was now spent on routine work, and as day after day passed by, I slowly began to set up more kidney Units, first Mutare in the north then in Harare, with Parirenyatwa the largest hospital in Zimbabwe once named the 'Alexandra Fleming Hospital' Followed by Central Hospital at Harare then Gweru Hospital in Central Zimbabwe, and finally Mpilo hospital Bulawayo, would provide a vast increase in health care provided for renal patients in the hospitals, in fact an extra fifty beds.

Slowly, yet still somewhat inconsistently at times I managed to carry out the work at each of the hospital's, the work was initially quite hard and time consuming, and the materials were extremely difficult to obtain, in fact it was not until long after I had completed the units, that I experienced more and more equipment and materials becoming available in the shops. Instead at the time of the installations I had been forced into a daily ritual of queuing at a variety of different builder's merchants. Most times for up to three hours just to obtain the single item they had in stock. Very often I had to join the staff searching through the piles of rusty fittings for what I needed. But at least it taught me perseverance.

Things were slowly improving and I managed to become involved in local interests, especially the church.

Also I was involved in a number of different ventures for Mr Moyo, things that I did not imagine I would ever become embroiled in.

Several occurrences that I shall never forget took place whilst I was living in Harare; the first of course had been my involvement in working within state house with all its security. At that time the Prime Minister's wife, Sally Mugabe, was suffering from kidney failure and the water that washed her blood, was unfortunately quite badly contaminated; my job had been to purify the water supplied to her machine.

At least three days a week I worked on the water samples from state house, and had to carry out minor alterations most weeks to their supply. One day I remember talking with her nurse, and expressing my personal thoughts, *"I am surprised how rude she is, being here three days of the week and never even speaking to me."*

It was the truth but very unprofessional for me to speak about it to the sister in charge of the unit.

The nurse left me, and within a few minutes Sally entered the plant room, on her knees, with her head down, *"Mr Clarredge, I am so sorry for being so rude, I did not mean to be."*

Dumbfounded I attempted a feasible response, *"Ma'am I did not intend you to hear my stupid remarks."*

Too late, for the very sick lady continued, *"You must have dinner with Bob* (Robert Mugabe) *and myself soon."*

My response, *"Thank you madam that would be lovely."*

I never had dinner with them, but ate regularly alone in a small dining room within State House. I soon discovered that Sally was a Christian, and had a very strong influence in guiding her husband at that time.

In fact looking back after her death and with her sound input gone, I guess if she had seen all that took place up to today, she would have wept at seeing her adopted country (Sally was Ghanaian) ruined.

History has proved time and time again, that, 'absolute power corrupts'.

Poverty does terrible things for the people that live under its dominance, and one of the nastier things that frightened me was a case of blackmail.

One Sunday afternoon there was a sharp rap on the door of my flat and to my surprise there was a Policeman, and a well-dressed black man, with a young girl of about ten years old. The man addressed me, *"This is your child and you haven't paid any upkeep for ten years."*

It would have been difficult, as I had only lived in Harare for six months. *"Unless you pay me I will report you, also for smuggling money into the country."* The policeman removed his handcuffs from his belt, and I professed to be a Christian and his source had been all lies. The child had disappeared in the confusion and after giving the man *(Stupidly)* the equivalent of 50p to leave me in peace she emerged from my bedroom, and left with the fellow.

Still stunned from the occurrence I discovered several things had been taken from my room including my transistor radio.

I expected to have seen the last of this so-called blackmailer, not so, for within a week and leaving by the private entrance of State House in my 'yellow peril', I saw him waiting in the road outside.

Sure enough that evening he turned up again, this time to claim I was working and selling the presidents medicines and he would report me.

A novel claim, but highly dangerous for me! I talked with Lino, a Portuguese friend whom I had come to know through business, I knew I could trust him for good advice, especially when situations like this came up, he had a perfect *ear* when I was experiencing times of trouble.

He told me how many white people were caught up in blackmail.

"*What can I do"?* I asked him.

He knew who I worked for and suggested I had a word with the secret police! This greatly concerned me, because it could well spell the blackmailers death sentence, and therefore gave added cause to be restrained in my approach.

I warned the blackmailers and for a short time I did not see them, unfortunately it started up again with even more outlandish threats, so I felt forced to do something. I had a word with the secret police and stressed that I didn't want anything nasty taking place to the culprits; *"Just warned off."*

Agreement was reached and I set up a meeting with the blackmailers at six o'clock in the evening at the 'Courtney Hotel'.

The secret police arrived; six in all, wearing long white

trench coats, dark glasses, and small but conspicuous homburg style hats. The shape of a gun could be seen resting in each man's shoulder holster!! Talk about gangster films of the thirties.

Needless to say my extortionist never turned up. After they received a polite dressing down from myself only one officer came to the re-arranged meeting the next night dressed in 'mufti'.

It turned out the blackmailer was attempting to make money for his sick child, and with a further gift and a threat never to see me again, the man moved back to the rural area, and I never saw him again.

CHAPTER 5

Missionary house Beira seafront

Whilst working in Harare, and until my radio was stolen I had been an avid listener to Radio 1, the Zimbabwean equivalent to the UK's BBC's Radio 4.

Over a number of weeks and during an assortment of my listening to my favourite programmes, I began to pick up snippets of news regarding the adjoining country which turned out to be Mozambique, it would not have taken a blind man very much time, to pick up on the heavily biased state-controlled news broadcast daily on ZBC, leaving no doubt in my mind that there was a full-sized civil war taking place between two separate factions each wanting to rule the country.

The main conflict had commenced since Mozambique had gained a particularly bloody and uncomfortable independence from Portugal, and this had escalated badly after President Samora Michel had died in a plane crash. (*He was great friend and supporter to Mr Mugabe*). This relationship had meant that the Zimbabwean army were available to fight for the Frelimo communist party.

The two factions in the conflict were the Marxist front for the liberation of Mozambique (FRELIMO) and the anti-communist insurgent forces of the Mozambique National resistance (RENAMO).

It was therefore a great shock to me when my telephone rang; and a man's voice asked if I might be free to go to Beira, "*to check our water supply in a missionary house we have purchased on the sea front.*" (What he had failed to mention was the dilapidated condition of the property, in fact half the back of the building had already fallen into the sea); '*We not only need fresh drinking water, but purified water for installing a printing press used for Christian tracts for the people.*" I felt it a strange request, for the 'Beira Corridor' as it was known in those days, was possibly the most dangerous road in the whole of sub-equatorial Africa.

I was in no doubt that if I accepted the request then it would mean taking my life in my hands.

Curiosity overcame any reservation that I felt, and I told Ron that I would be prepared to go.

I visited the Mozambique High Commission office in Harare and spent a few hours sorting out my visa, and then arranged with my office that I should be away for three days.

They were not too pleased, for Pat had arranged a ticket and visa on the previous month for me to fly into Mozambique and visit a client for hers, I had got to the airport only to find that the 'Air Mozambique' plane had left a day early!

I felt sure because of this occurrence that it was not God's will for me to go on my own at that time, and He had shut the door.

The all-important day quickly arrived and putting a change of clothes in a small suitcase, I walked the short distance to Ron's house.

The time was six o'clock in the morning, and when the vehicle turned up I was surprised to find that I was not alone with Ron, for there were a further six people in the mini bus heading to our destination, what I didn't realise was the great distance, nearly 600 Kilometres, and an eight-hour journey ahead of me.

My job on this first trip to Beira was to watch for the telltale signs of booby traps; these I was told would be in the form of landmines. Admittedly I had never seen a modern mine, although I had seen many of the ex-World War Two round iron mines with their pointed tentacles sitting outside the lifeboat stations in England collecting money for the RNLI (*The Royal National Lifeboat Institution*), I had no experience of modern warfare, So I knew this would be a great challenge.

We stopped for coffee in the beautiful town of Mutare on the Zimbabwe border. I had lovely memories of this small city where I had fitted a kidney unit in the city hospital, and quite recently had a growth successfully removed from my scalp by Mr Kitcat one of the surgeons.

As I have said previously the surface of the highway as we entered Mozambique had turned out to be catastrophic, for within a kilometre of entering the country I had a taste of its deficiencies, the potholes we encountered strongly resembled three to four metre bomb craters, and most of these were filled to the top with water, a natural phenomenon as it was the rainy season.

The depth of these depressions were mostly inconceivable, that is with the exception of one long trench that we passed, no more than a few kilometres down the road from the Zimbabwe border. There we saw a ten-tonne lorry with its bonnet buried in the ground some three four feet below the road surface; from that point on in our journey I knew there could be no lapse on my vigilance.

"*Mines could be placed in the potholes*," our driver informed me, "*be careful.*"

This particular driver seemed to have no fear of death, for he drove like mad on the uneven road, the tension increased as did my flow of adrenalin many times over, I saw strange shapes on the road surface, which I had never seen in my life before; and now I was totally exhausted. After travelling for at least ninety-seven Kilometres on the dangerous road and severely straining my eyes in the process of preventing our transport from being grounded or blown up by any of the strangely camouflaged traps I felt mentally exhausted.

I was thankful when we came to a town and stopped to have a flask of coffee.

The city was called Chimoio and the first thing I noticed were the huge hoardings that declared the benefits provided by the communist government. The second thing I observed, and by far much more serious, were the large number of children wearing old sacking to cover their naked bodies, holes and torn material indicated the lack of everyday items, whilst a number of children without legs moved on their buttocks through the streets. My heart went out to them, as it did my wife a year or so later when she visited the area.

Not far after leaving the city we passed through a heavily wooded area were Ron pointed out a gateway which was almost hidden between the tall cedar trees, *"this is the entrance to a house where some friends of mine live, they are from Zimbabwe, Roy and Trish, they have a farm and orange grove were they are looking after orphaned children."*

Sadly at that time we were far too busy in our attempt to reach Beira before darkness, to allow time to visit the orphanage, yet if I had known then that Lilian and myself would have a wonderful opportunity to help them in the future.

Eventually we arrived in Beira, which I could only describe as an eye-opener. It had much wider streets than any other town that we had passed through, but most ended as suddenly as we had entered them, due to the huge crater holes in their surface prohibiting access.

No road signs of any description were apparent; in fact, the road to the seafront where the Missionary House lay was quite precarious to say the least, the street on which the house was situated was called Mouzinho De Albuquerque Rua, and with Ron's excellent knowledge of the City we soon found it.

Instead of potholes we were now looking to see if any other immediate dangers were in the vicinity; thankfully not.

Politics seems to be the main adversary in so many African states. If we are honest nothing has changed throughout history.

Jesus spoke of wars in Matthew 24; verse 6 (King James

Version), *"And ye shall hear of wars and rumours of war."*

Once we had arrived at the house I was surprised to see such a large structure and at first sight found it extremely difficult to give a fair description of the property.

From the front it looked magnificent that was apart from the poor condition of its paintwork, in fact I assumed it was either the salty air or lack of cash flow by the previous owner that had left the walls starved of paint. I felt sad at the condition that I now saw the building in, and visualized what it would have been like when first built.

The whole dwelling had been constructed on the beautiful, picture-book white sandy beach and was standing less than five metres back from the Indian Ocean. The picturesque limpet strewn rocks, formed breakers that induced perfectly shaped waves, as they cascaded upon the sand, the clear blue water lapping towards the property.

On reaching the back of the house I was flabbergasted at what I saw, for As I wrote earlier in this chapter, the ocean had taken the foundations and destroyed a great deal of the back wall, Ron had formulated a plan to save the structure which involved a scheme to place large rocks covered in barbed wire at the rear of the house. I never fully understood how this could work.

My job primarily, was to put drinkable water into this property, at that moment through problems with Beira's water purification works, the whole city had been robbed of its once reliable and uncontaminated water supply. In fact it was doubtful if any substantial and safe supply would be available till after the war was over.

From the moment I saw the state of the structure I felt it

was a waste of money. In fact a year or so later when my wife was with me a Welsh bricklayer had given up his holiday and flown out to Beira, he was attempting to rebuild the wall, it was evident that he too shared our views as every brick he laid he muttered the words, *"Unscriptural, building a house upon the sand."*

Once I had carried out a thorough survey of the house and listed their requirements I asked if I might visit the city hospital and see how they compared to the ones in which I worked in Zimbabwe.

One of the workers was given the job of taking me to Centro Hospitalar Cova da Beira, thankfully the hospital was very close to our location. Once we had arrived I could not fail to see a queue of at least 200 raggedly dressed people, each appeared to be holding a tin or jar of some sort in their hands. As we passed the front of the queue I observed a single tap, from this it was easy to see that it gave only the smallest of drips, which must have taken an age to fill even a cup.

My guide explained that this was untreated water straight from the Indian Ocean and would have been collected by visitors for a relative who was a patient in the hospital.

Feeling totally devastated by what I had seen, we continued on till we came to the main entrance of the hospital.

Once we entered the dry and dusty access to the building I was shaken to see it was filled with scores of people, aimlessly standing in the hot airless lobby. Without wasting any further time my colleague and I went across to a small desk, behind which was seated a grey uniformed lady who would not have looked out of place as a prison warden of the 1800s. I did not know Portuguese so I could not understand the call she made on the telephone. A few minutes later, a much smarter and happier looking, well-proportioned woman entered the lobby; my guide introduced me to the lady, who turned out to be the matron. Her name was Matilda and her English impeccable, she had recently returned from further training at Manchester in the UK.

She had become a Christian whilst in England and had returned with her newfound faith; she certainly needed it, as she took me personally around the large 2,000 bedded hospital telling me that she was praying for help to save people's lives.

Paint starved and grubby would have been a gross understatement of its condition. We commenced our visit in the large maternity ward. To enter it, we had to duck beneath one of the largest spiders web's I had ever seen in my life; looking up after passing the web; I caught my breath at what I saw; for it was a bird eating spider, this particular arachnid had a span of no less than six inches and an evil face that seemed to be looking directly at me. I don't mind spiders but I did make this one an exception.

Once in the ward I faced another shock for each bed I could see held two prospective mothers, whilst below on a thin mattress were a further two patients.

That was bad enough, but quite suddenly a large black rat followed by its children rushed into the ward, running full pelt over a number of patients, I was horrified. Matilda must have seen my face for she instantly ushered me out of the ward and into the main hospital; dirt and grime everywhere, *"We have no water and very little food."*

I had heard through the news in Zimbabwe that people were starving in Mozambique, and this confirmed all that I had heard.

My heart went out to these poor people and without hesitation I turned to Matilda and said, *"I will get water on for the hospital."*

What had I promised? I asked myself, certainly what on the surface seemed to be the impossible.

Every ward we visited appeared to be worse than the previous one, and by the time I had to return to Harare, I knew exactly what had to be done to give them a fresh water supply. One thing that greatly upset me was a shop that I had seen in the centre of Beira City, which appeared to be full of every commodity from Coca Cola to television sets. Virtually anything that money could buy. Whilst there, I had stopped and entered it, only to be told that the only currency accepted was the American Dollar, I had no dollars so I had to leave the shop with nothing, as did the vast majority of people.

The journey back to Harare was very long and on the way we stopped at the orange farm to meet Roy and Trish; They turned out to be a lovely couple, we were also introduced to their helpers; following this we met the children; they were delightful and of all ages; although sadly a large number of them did not speak because we were told they had been traumatised. This had taken place when the 'bandits' had captured their parents. Evidently the little children, many under five years of age, had been left to find their own 'salvation'. Miraculously many of these children had travelled hundreds of kilometres without any knowledge of this haven, yet ended up here; meaning now they were cared for and could live in comparative safety.

We then shared in a meal, strangely I was not told its content until I had eaten it, it turned out to be a small fragment of python, a protected snake that had been killed, (*understandably because they were starving)*, and each day they had used a foot of it to feed the children. *"In case you wonder it tasted like chicken."*

I was shown around the farm and viewed the nicely decorated rooms the children shared with their helpers. The farm was extensive and the orange grove magnificent, all to quickly our time came to an end, as we had to beat the closing of the border gate with Zimbabwe. With great sincerity I promised to visit them again when I returned to Mozambique; Ron left them some food and almost immediately we left for Harare.

On my return I could not forget the thousand or so patients at the hospital, plus the countless children on the streets begging for help. Remembering as a Christian I was now committed as I had made a promise to help, and however impossible it seemed, it had to be my bond in Christ's name.

CHAPTER 6

Throop United Reformed Church

Within three weeks I had returned to the UK for a month's leave, and to face the challenge of getting water into Beira hospital over 9,000 miles away.

On my return home Lil and I met in a house group from Throop United Reformed Church at which I had shared my concerns for Beira Hospital. The year was 1987 and Roger our house group leader suggested that we might set up a charity to provide the money for the water purification system that I had promised and would be suitable to alleviate many of the problems I had recently encountered in Mozambique.

"The name could be Rivers of living water?"

I agreed, and he proposed that we should set up a bank account to cover the costs.

A very practical idea and immediately I set too in raising the necessary finance to purchase the equipment. I wrote to every church within a thirty-mile radius from where I lived, and asked for the sum of £5. The response was good and within a couple of weeks I had enough money to buy a very basic water plant: and I then had to find a manufacturer from whom I could purchase all the equipment that I needed.

I found the storage tanks and pumps at a factory near Bristol plus enough bacterium (*Water cleaning maggots*) required to purify the water. These were in stock and I managed to purchase them quite easily. With the remaining funds, I succeeded in obtaining a powerful pump plus a number of wash-hand basins, and all the plumbing items to fit them into the system in both the hospital and Missionary House.

Having purchased virtually every item I should need, my next job and certainly the most important was how to get it to Beira?

I contacted Ron who was also on leave in the UK, and his suggestion was that we try Tearfund which was based in Teddington near Richmond, Surrey and covered distribution to a large part of the underprivileged world as their service for the Lord; perhaps they could ship the equipment for me?

To my excitement my shipment was accepted, although all too quickly I received a dampener to my spirit as I was told it could take between three months and a year to arrive. I thought of all the lives that the equipment would save and the number of deaths if the shipment were delayed.

I had no other choice than to take it to their distribution

centre, which I believe at that time was near Sevenoaks in Kent, although my memory is a little hazy.

The BBC filmed my donation as it left my house in Christchurch, my how I prayed that the life-giving equipment would arrive much earlier than I had been told.

Within a few days I was back on Air Zimbabwe returning to Harare and my work, even on the day I arrived at six thirty in the morning; my enthusiasm breached any tiredness, for within thirty-five minutes from landing I was back, working in Parirenyatwa hospital and on the kidney ward.

My work in Zimbabwe could never be called routine and working at State House gave me a number of privileges that others white workers were not given, including the use of Mr Mugabe's elderly Mercedes car, I had never driven one of these cars until that time and on driving it through the city to get some plumbing fixtures I was stopped at one of the many police road blocks; the officer holding a large clip board in his hand curtly challenged me, *"Your road tax is out of date."*

His face was a picture when I gave him the address of the car owner and his panic was obvious, as he quickly waved me on.

Hatfield church was going to have a social evening and I was due to cook the meat, it was minced goat, and enough for at least thirty people; I filled a large number of black pots and carefully wrapped them in blankets; in an endeavour to keep them warm for with the fairly heavy Harare traffic I guessed the journey would be at least half an hour in length.

The Yellow Peril started and I drove it along King George Road for about five hundred yards before I joined the long queue of waiting vehicles, it was obvious that I had been stopped by what had now become a traditional police check.

Eventually I reached the block and was told very politely to switch the engine off; I explained it might not start again, but my comment was totally ignored, and through this, I immediately encountered a bigger problem as once checked and cleared, the vehicle refused to start again!

Turning to the officer in charge I addressed him, *"It's your fault, you told me to turn the engine off."*

I held up an ever-growing line of cars, *"I have the food in my car to feed a church at Hatfield, what are you going to do about it?"*

I noticed the man as I looked inside my window and by his reactions picked up the very strong odour of the meat.

Somewhat unfair on my part, but it was not their fault, but in that era there was still a great deal of respect for most white people that had remained loyal to the new regime; and after stressing my position; and whom I worked for, I certainly received special treatment.

I have always found the Zimbabwe police to be extremely polite and on this occasion I was not disappointed, as following a discussion between the officers, one of the men picked up a chain and attached firstly to the police car and then to my car; I was then towed along the road for several hundred yards to see if my car started, it did. However the kindly policemen said he was afraid the car might stop so he would follow me.

The journey was for nearly five miles and once we arrived at the church, the officer willingly joined in the meal; on the surface he appeared to really enjoy the Christian fellowship. I must add that I did question his motives, but perhaps I am being a little too suspicious.

Many incidents occurred over the next few weeks and I had a marvellous opportunity on national radio to take part in a science programme with Colin Harvey.

During the programme I felt a small voice in my mind telling me to ask for a lift to Beira two weeks from that very day; I fought the urge to broadcast my request for at least twenty minutes, until I succumbed to the 'small voice', *"If anybody could give me a lift to Beira and…"*

I shared the date that was totally clear within my brain, believing this message to be from God.

The studio response was instant as the producer stormed into the studio telling me in no uncertain terms that personal business was not allowed on the public broadcasting service!! I wilted under his forceful subjugation and for a short period kept well away from ZBC.

Three calls came into the studio for me; the first two were people wanting 'Prawns' if I could get them, *(The reason behind this was the quality of the sea food and prior to the war, the weekend treat for many Zimbabwean's had been to drive to Beira and enjoy its gastronomic finesse)*. The third call was the best, for a lady, who's name I failed to get, promised to pay for an aircraft belonging to missionary aviation to fly me into Beira airport.

I lost no time in booking the plane, and set about preparing for the trip, I quickly got my visa, and arranged accommodation with an American missionary that lived in the city.

Five days prior to leaving, I had a disturbing call from the airport saying the lady had not paid, and as I was not supported by a church organization they were unable to take me.

My natural response had been, *"How do I get there?"*

The male voice with a Canadian accent on the line instantly suggested, *"Hitch hike."*

I knew a few vehicles travelled the road, but it was so dangerous that it was mainly the familiar 'diamond' shaped army lorries of the Zimbabwe forces that travelled the route and I was certain they would not be allowed to give me a lift.

I explained this to the fellow and He responded with an impossible suggestion, *"Hitch hike on a plane at Charles Prince Airport in the Western suburbs."* I was absolutely devastated, and started to question the strong impulse I had felt within my brain, yet knowing in myself it had to have been God speaking to me. Nothing could convince me it otherwise, and I was still certain that I should still go.

Waving all caution aside I locked up my flat on the day in question and took a small bag of clothes plus some sandwiches and two tins of *'Stone's Ginger beer'* my favourite non-alcoholic beverage.

I ordered an A1 taxi to take me to the airport and on my arrival could not fail to see the large number of small aircraft in front of an even greater number of hangers.

The runway ran parallel to the road with a small fence restricting access from the road. The strong smell of the numerous hibiscus plants set off my hay fever.

Nervously I stood next to the runway, closing my eyes in a psychological attempt to convince myself that I could not be seen, I raised my hand in the time honoured way of thumbing a lift.

Within moments, a large hand rested upon my shoulders causing me to jump, I turned and looked up into the face of the owner of the hands, it was a very tall gentleman with a strong American accent. He politely addressed me, *"I'm Hank who are you."*

I oftentimes wondered afterwards if perhaps he thought I was demented, certainly it would have been quite natural. *"Alan,"* I simply replied.

He then asked: *"What are you doing?"*

Thinking it was rather an obvious question I responded, *"Thumbing a lift."*

There was a short pause before he said, *"where too?"*

"Beira!" I replied.

"Beira. You know there's a civil war going on there?"

Shrugging my shoulders in response to his words, I acquiesced. Leaving him in no doubt that I already knew.

"Who sent you there?" he asked.

Taking the bull by the horns I said, *"I believe it was God."*

Without any further questions for the moment, the fellow that now faced me looked very thoughtful, then he addressed me and without hesitation said, *"If God has told you then I will take you."*

My heart leapt with joy as he continued to explain that he was from 'World Vision' and had booked the same plane as I had previously ordered. (*God does move in mysterious ways.*)

They were going to another part of Mozambique but were quite happy to drop me off at Beira, *"And we will pick you up three days later at the airport."*

Walking to the airstrip I told him of the work I had planned within the hospital and the Missionary House.

The flight was particularly interesting for me, for I was seated next to the pilot; from time to time whilst we were flying over the Mozambican air space I saw what appeared to be a number of fairly small, black clouds some distance below us, to me it appeared to be either smoke, or tiny rain clouds, strange as it seemed to come from nowhere.

"What are those clouds, rain?" I asked the pilot.

"No, gun fire."

I froze in my seat; recognising my concern he wasted no time in allaying my fears by explaining the situation to me, *"Don't worry their guns don't have enough fire power to reach our height, so they are just wasting their ammo."*

My concern immediately evaporated and shutting my ears to the droning of the noisy engine I sat back in the comfortable seat and against all odds fell into a deep sleep.

When we arrived at Beira airport I could easily see from the planes porthole that the whole complex was deserted, with the exception of a large number of rusty army lorries on its perimeter. Alongside these vehicles appeared to be a military base which was easily distinguishable by a large number of what could only have been described as Nissan huts, this was made even more obvious by the typically high watch towers, each with an armed guard pointing his gun in our direction, a bit disconcerting but not unexpected during a civil war.

Not a single aircraft in was in sight; so different than the airfield I had just left. Before leaving the aircraft, Hank prayed with me and gave me a sum of money to pay airport fees and anything I might have to pay out. I had forgotten these and praised God I was totally under his care and protection.

The final words Hank said greatly blessed me, *"We will be*

praying for you every day and will be back in three days' time to collect you."

Alone I entered the spacious, yet empty customs hall, the inspection was only cursory, and in less than two minutes, I found myself standing in the large gloomy entrance hall of Beira Airport.

I certainly had a good reason for feeling alone. Outside of the terminal building I could distinctly hear the ominous sound of firearms and incendiary bombs exploding in the nearby streets.

I had not visualised being stuck in this terminal building with no transport or food until Hank and World Vision collected me.

That fear was quickly quashed, for within five or ten minutes a Red Cross ambulance arrived to pick up a patient, there was no patient! Instead it turned out to be my God provided transport; and within twenty minutes I was at the Hospital and only a short walking distance to my accommodation at an American Missionary's house.

That night completely unknown to me a cargo ship had arrived at the docks from the UK, On board all of my equipment. Gods timing is the best!!!

CHAPTER 7

With great excitement, both on my part and judging by the reactions of the dismally dressed hospital staff, who were happily serenading as they worked alongside me.

There was certainly a great atmosphere of anticipation which was reflected by their beautiful singing, as each member of staff delicately handled the equipment that had been unloaded from the ship; every item appeared to be intact with the exception of one washbasin, which was smashed and had been intended for use within the Missionary House; every other piece of apparatus was in perfect condition. Praise the Lord!!

Although my time was extremely short before returning to Zimbabwe I managed to fix at least one new tap into the existing well-water supply, and by attaching a very basic filtration system and a small pump it would help considerably, thankfully all this equipment had been on the recent shipment.

I knew that in some way, however small the flow of water, it would be a large increase from just a dripping tap. The descent flow from the well would help, if only a little for the 2,000 patients until I returned to the hospital.

After some quite hard, and difficult negotiating with Ron; he managed to allow me to use his bricklayer and also one labourer; this was quite a sacrifice on his part for up till that point they had been working on the Missionary House and this would delay the completion of the house by several weeks at the least.

I purchased enough bricks and mortar from a local Christian building firm and they also agreed to deliver everything to the hospital, thankfully I had some British pounds, which were readily accepted.

Whilst I was back in Zimbabwe the tradesman with his helpers, would now be able to continue building a brick edifice to hold the new water purification plant.

Because of the internal war that was taking place this new structure had to be securely locked and made tamperproof: then at least this would afford protection of the system from saboteurs; its roof tanks would also have to be under cover if only to protect the pure water storage from vermin. It was not unknown for rats under normal conditions to enter the tanks by eating through the polythene covers, then falling in the water and drowning. It was protection against not just the four-legged beasts, but also against assassins that could put poison in the supply, killing all who drank the water. The need for security was uppermost in my mind, as I carried out the planning and I was reminded of several years previous to my coming to Zimbabwe, when I *'received'* an invitation to a once secret Government research centre near Milton Keynes in the UK. *(Supposedly for a works social of an American company whom I had supplied information regarding their water treatment plants.)* The secrecy that surrounded this supposed ex-army base was absolute; with a total ban on aircraft flying over it at any time.

The nine or so cars which arrived with me, were checked by army officers holding mirrors under each of the vehicles; evidently to check for bombs. When completed, I was mystified, as each one of us was requested to sign the Official Secrets Act. After this, a number of army outriders surrounded us, then a staff car drew up to the front, and a military vehicle pulled up at the back of our short convoy. We were immediately escorted to the main building, which stood to the rear of a large parade ground. I could clearly see the parade ground was no longer in use, for numerous tufts of grass could be seen growing through numerous cracks on the surface, once inside the old MOD Building (*Ministry of Defence*) I noticed that there were about thirty of us in attendance, and before having any form of conversation we were all quickly seated in the front reception area.

Quite suddenly a *'nightmare'* took place and the noise of klaxons, small detonations and whistles became apparent; as across the parade ground a number of dark lorries with headlights fully on and dazzling floodlights on their cab roofs, even in daylight, it was extremely effective, plus every vehicles also had its horn blaring. The speed that they descended upon us was phenomenal; it was very noticeable that every one of us in unison stood to our feet; I guess like myself they would have been totally confused. From the lorries a number of men alighted shouting at the top of their voices, opened mouthed I watched as with their rifles raised they smashed the glass front doors and at least twenty black hooded men entered the area in which we stood. A number of them held a large rope, these fellows surrounded us, and before our shock had subsided; pulled us tightly together, we were well and truly captured, the frightening experience was brought to a halt quite swiftly, as from the roof a man dressed as 007 James Bond shinned down a rope to the musical theme from the recent film '*Moonraker*'.

This was our induction to the most serious of lectures that I have ever attended in my life, and to this day have never divulged their content, as a water engineer I had been chosen to attend to learn about my role in any purposeful attempt to poison the water supplies of Britain, not just me but also the others that had joined us for this day.

Although to lighten our newfound liabilities, we had some exciting diversions, such as using a skid pad, and travelling at one hundred miles an hour in a driverless car, on a race track (*Totally unknown to the public in those days, or to any of us*). The main reason for the conference had all to quickly become as apparent, and I learnt how easy it would be to kill the population of London, Birmingham or any city or township in the United Kingdom.

All this had left me prepared for the worse, hence the security of the hospital water tanks in Beira.

The main supply of power would be through solar panels which would be the only items on view, it was decided, these would have to be mounted on a metal pole and at least 10 metres from the ground; this I felt would be the safest place and the mast secured tightly. I had designed the complete system to give ample water and with the correct 'bugs', Ultra violet rays and filtration there would be little chance of cholera or typhoid, not only that but also the excellent storage capacity for the 2,000 patients plus the staff would be met.

Because of its intense urgency the bricklayer promised to start work immediately on the foundations, and Ron agreed to bring me down in fourteen days' time to work on the new system.

On the Sunday night I was asked to speak at the local Baptist church (*with an interpreter*).

I so enjoyed the uplifting experience, for the church was absolutely packed with people praising God and singing the wonderful hymns, only one slip up, and that was mine, for on the platform end was the baptistery without a cover, and being a walking type of preacher I accidently caught the edge of the huge bath, and literally fell in. I shall remember the gasp from the congregation up till this day.

I was thankful that there was no water in it, although it would have been a much softer fall if it had been full. Of course the town was without a sound water supply, so any clean water would have been drunk dry long ago by the Pastor and his congregation, as were the local swimming pools by their owners.

After the service I was invited to join the Pastors and congregation in a *'Prayer March.'* The route chosen would pass though the centre of the city; and was to show the Russian oppressor's that dominated Beira; that they were no longer wanted; and to pray they might leave their city.

I shall never forget the poignant experience as several hundred people moved slowly through the main street watched by the local inhabitants; many of the folks were on sticks, a number were even legless caused through the numerous minefields around the city. I remember picking a blind child out of a drain, as most of the grills were broken and a hazard to be missed; at one point somebody came out of a block of flats and asked if we could pray for a little baby that was dangerously ill; we entered the flat and laid hands and prayed over the child I heard at a later date that the little girl, who I believe through her mother's faith, had been healed, Praise the Lord!!!!

The march finished at a big building in the city, which I had been told was the Russian Embassy; The Russians were totally disliked because of their bullying influence over the communist Mozambique government; not only that, but they were also taking the wealth out of the country, adding to the problem was their large demand for food for their military personal.

Everybody joined hands and we formed a circle around the house; strangely the barrel of a huge gun outside the embassy pointed towards the building, instead of the Indian Ocean before it.

The praying was spontaneous and extremely determined. Admittedly I felt extremely nervous.

There was no need, for the very next day the Russians, and their army lorries, filled with soldiers, moved out of Beira for good. I had now witnessed with my own eyes, and on this occasion once more, the power of prayer and that God has control over every situation, even countries as powerful as the Soviet Union, whatever size they are, and irrespective of their politics! For these dear people of Beira, God had once again answered prayer!!

As promised I was picked up at the airport and safely returned to Harare the next day; I had witnessed more than one miracle on this trip, but to me because of my calling, the greatest had been the miracle of the arrival of the equipment. The ship, according to the captain, had arrived within six weeks of its dispatch from the UK, at least ten days shorter journey than normal, the mighty way that God had brought me to Beira by the original plane, at the right time; and with the ambulance to the right place; The impossible also made possible by the customs officials, for they had cleared it within two hours, and now just two days on, the bricklayers had commenced their work; I now knew that God had been right; this was nothing less than conformation of the decision made back in my days at Christchurch Baptist Church.

Once back to my normal work I spent time preparing each of the six major renal units to function perfectly, and then at each unit praying with the staff that all would be well, before taking my official leave. At each unit I explained that I would be away for at least six weeks.

Just over a week after returning to Harare I asked John Baker the pastor; of '*Eastlea AOG*' in Harare if he could drive me to Beira to check on the building work; he readily agreed and with my contacts in the health service we managed to stay in Mutare Hospital medical accommodation for a night, this was at least some distance towards our destination and would enable us to make an early start as soon as the customs post opened.

I slept well, but poor John didn't, the reason, one that didn't worry me, was because a beautiful tarantula spider was on the wall above his bed.

After a good breakfast we took the notorious road to our destination, at my suggestion we decided to make a break and visit the orange farm on our way to Beira, the weather was sunny and the leafy green drive leading to the orphanage was almost hidden from view, this allowed us to reach the emerald pasture which we could easily observe yet unseen from the highway. The grove was filled with hundreds of ripe, fruit laden trees; the almost blood red oranges weighed the branches down, yet still allowed our car to pass safely beneath.

It was very strange for the place appeared to be completely deserted. Pulling up in front of the long frontage of the single-storey building, I immediately noticed its large cross, signifying its saving work, although the lack of life seemed an enigma in a thriving children's home.

It was far more than a mere puzzle, for looking at the surroundings of the bungalow my attention was drawn to the surface of the ground and what appeared to be large mound of dried grass, this heap of what I took to be silage was placed at the top of a fairly steep incline, which stretched the length of the house and even beyond; as we looked, the nearest pile to where we were standing could be seen moving and quite suddenly I saw a small head appear between its tufts, followed by another and then several more children.

Soon the child minders also emerged and after shaking off the loose foliage from their clothes they set about removing the light wooden slats that, beneath the grass, covered their hideaway.

Now standing beside the underground shelter I watched as Trish helped a further fifteen children that had been hidden from view out of the now completely open trench.

Trish explained that the 'bandits' had raided the farm just a few hours previously and their only means of escape had been, by rolling the children out of the side doors and into the long ditch which was always left ready to hide.

In the past there had been a major raid; and at that time; the lack of preparation or expectation meant that no shelter had been built; on this occasion most of the staff had been kidnapped, amongst those at the orphanage was an eighty-year-old English woman. These became prisoners and were forced to walk hundreds of miles on a meagre diet, only being set free six months later when the Danish diplomats had cleverly negotiated their release.

In this case the children had been safely rolled through the side and back doors and been hidden in this simplistic yet practical shelter then been covered by straw.

Inside the house we could easily see large holes in the walls and lots of bullet marks, Both John and I came to the conclusion that we should abandon our trip to Beira.

Then we received a shock for Roy asked us which direction we had entered the farm from? John explained and I instantly saw his face. *"You crossed a small army minefield?"*

As if to confirm his statement I saw the familiar uniforms of the Zimbabwe army emerging from the trees, it was just a small group of men yet I had the distinct feeling of safety at their presence.

Immediately Roy spoke to the officer in charge and judging by their hand movements and symmetry, they left the soldiers in no doubt of our predicament.

The Zimbabwean soldiers and their officers had been well

trained by the British army and without wasting any further time formulated a scheme.

This entailed six soldiers; four marched in front of our car with pointed test rods. Then one on each side of the vehicle, each man wore an earpiece which had been attached to their rods.

It was unfortunate, but it turned out that the officer did not have any access to plans of the minefield. So a nerve-racking undertaking took place, as each soldier prodded the ground around our car; very slowly and extremely carefully, in fact at walking pace we were able to retrace our route, returning over the grassy surface beneath our car.

Through this visit I now knew the main essentials required to run their organization and decided to put my knowledge to the test, both in obtaining the goods; and then deciding on the priority of each item that would help them best.

This would include supplying everything they had asked for, which even included school uniforms; the pupils of Epiphany Church School a short distance from my Bournemouth home in Dorset gave these.

This whole procedure of crossing the minefield took far too long and knowing that the gate between Mozambique and Zimbabwe shut its doors at eight o' clock; we made the decision to head for home earlier. Beira would have to wait a few days; but also, I knew the new challenge at the orphanage had become another work for the Lord.

Within four hours we had crossed the border and returned to the comparative safety of Zimbabwe.

CHAPTER 8

'Grande Hotel 1987'

It was the Friday morning of the following week, and keeping true to our arrangements, Ron arrived at my flat to pick me up. It was barely 5.00 a.m. in the morning and he appeared to be bright and bursting to go.

"A nice early start," had been his words.

Being an early bird I was also packed and ready to go. Once again I was to place my life into his hands, and face the nail-biting road leading to Beira. We prayed for safety and immediately left the courtyard of No 2 Capri Court Avondale, driving through the city along Samora Michel and onto the high road to Mutare, next we crossed the Mozambique border check, and did not stop again until we had reached the safety of the dilapidated Missionary House on the seafront. I admired the stamina and zeal of Ron in his vision for that war torn country.

Unfortunately by the time we arrived it was very late in the afternoon, and I could only take a cursory glance at the work. It was difficult and quite complicated but with a strong will I arranged to commence the next day.

It was then that Ron dropped the bombshell, *"We haven't got any accommodation available in the house, but there is an old caravan on the beach, which has a bed in it."*

I am not a fussy person normally where accommodation is concerned, especially some of the places I have had to go for the Lord's work, but on consideration I felt I would have to be at death's door before using that particular bug infested van. *(If only I had known the part it played in my future I think I might have lost my nerve, and gone home).*

I decided to take the ball into my own court and to try to sort out my own accommodation.

I took the short walk to the hospital, where the officious looking secretary that I had met on my previous visit listened intently as I told her I needed help in finding lodgings. It was immediately apparent that she understood me, for the woman instantly made a telephone call, and it was evident by her expression she had received a positive response; I watched as she removed a large pad from a drawer beneath her desk and explained in perfect English that she was to issue a requisition note, *"And I will now call a hotel to see if they have a room for you."*

After she had confirmed they had the room, she held further debate over what appeared to be quite a touchy subject; would the hotel take a government payment? It became evident by her mannerisms that it would. She completed the form without any further delay, only confirming its validity, with a very noisy swipe of the Government stamp of approval.

Then calling a young man dressed in a threadbare uniform over to her desk, the lady told him something in Portuguese. Turning to me she explained in perfect English; *"We are putting you up in the 'Grande Hotel' Philippe will take you."*

"Thank you," I responded. In my mind I felt extremely uneasy in allowing a bankrupt country, with starving people to pay for me in such a 'Swanky' sounding hotel, even the cheapest rooms would have done for a few days.

Once rounding the corner and experiencing the smell of rotting garbage in the streets and facing the high iron gates at the side entrance of my accommodation, my opinion changed; for from the very first moment that I saw the hotel, I must admit to it being quite a shock; any other description would have been a gross understatement of the facts.

However in its favour I could see that it had once been extremely prestigious building, not these days, for the ravages of war upon the tall building had left it looking virtually derelict, it had no glass in its windows and due to the city generator having been blown up, there was no electricity supply.

After signing in at the reception and giving in my passport; I was informed that my room was not yet ready; *"But might be available in two hours."*

I decided to visit an English-speaking local Pastor whom I had met earlier at the Missionary House.

His name was Joel certainly a very biblical name, I told him the reason why I was there in Beira and he invited me to join him for a short prayer time, primarily his emphasis was to ask for God's blessing on the work, but also a faith request that God would provide food for the tens of thousands of starving people in the city.

I soon discovered why he had prayed that particular request, for after returning to the hotel in the early evening and finding my room was available; I looked at the distinct lack of daylight and combined with this, a power cut; I decided to eat before going to my room. Entering the restaurant I was somewhat taken aback, as I noticed just how few guests were there, (a*bout six people in number, and these were all dressed in military uniforms*) each person appeared to carry an identical small paper bag in their hand which I correctly assumed was army issue? It didn't take me long to discover the reason; for this hotel; evidently typical of every hotel or guest house remaining in the city; had neither food nor drink and every visitor had to find their own supply.

Tired and hungry I gave up trying to amuse myself on the pool table in the huge and very empty 'games room', and as there was no electricity, I decided it was time to go to my accommodation.

I climbed the most dangerous staircase I had ever seen in my life; certainly worse than those that I had experienced in my wildest nightmares.

Unfortunately if I wanted to sleep I had no choice for it was absolutely necessary to climb ever flight of stairs in the hotel to reach my room. I had been accommodated on the top floor, risky would have been a gross understatement, not only because I suffer from night blindness, and by this time there had been very little daylight left; even more hazardous was the complete lack of any form of bannister; in fact, nothing whatsoever to indicate the edge of the concrete stairs and prevent any person from falling over the edge. The stairway was partially tiled and so uneven that I was almost petrified, ending up attempting to cling to a very rusty and broken in many places, hand rail attached to the internal wall of the stairwell (*the farthest point from the edge*) as I commenced to climb.

Ever since that day I have had a recurring nightmare, which I have woken up from many times experiencing the traumatic feeling of tumbling down for at least four stories before ending up in the basement and inevitable death.

Thankfully, I had brought a small torch with me, and all would have been well, had I not painfully caught the uneven edge of the top step that led to the gallery on which my room was situated with my big toe.

The torch rolled out of my hand and dropped to the first step; it was a well-made and sturdy little torch and the fall had no effect whatsoever on the bulb for its light remained undimmed and for a moment I was quite thankful thinking I could retrieve it.

Certainly, a false hope, for its descent became much faster, so fast that even an Olympic runner could not have achieved its capture; certainly judging by the noise of each step as it dropped to the next, and the erratic jumping of its illumination I surmised that it must have hit every step until it reached the floor beneath.

Then in awe I watched as the light rolled over the edge of the stairs and keeping as far away as was possible from the edge I observed it for as long as it was possible to follow, transfixed with dismay I eventually saw it fall to the depths below, its beam could be seen twisting in the air until it completely disappeared from my view, I did hear a muffled clatter as it hit the deck, and I remember hoping that no unsuspecting visitor or staff member were beneath its path.

No choice left but to find my bed, it was so dark now I decided to leave my clothes on the floor and ignore the ants and other small insects that I surmised were sharing my room, I could always shake them out of my clothes in the daylight.

It was time to lie down, this I did, but quite admittedly I felt selfish in feeling sorry for myself, certainly as a huge number of people were without food and starving to death at that time, unfortunately it was only six o'clock in the evening. But nature being as it is I knew I had been forced to take an early night. I dreaded having to be in my room, but knew I had no logical choice; I was still awake two hours later, and by this time I had got somewhat accustomed to the darkness I could make out the shape of a large bay window; as far as I could tell it was completely glassless as was the glazing in the lower levels of the hotel, yet the heat in my room was completely unbearable. I guessed it was through one hundred percent humidity. Although that could not take all the credit, for its huge mosquito population that bit every part of my body played a great part; sadly, there were no mosquito nets.

I had no idea of the time, when quite unexpectedly I heard loud voices on the landing outside my room. Without warning the door suddenly burst open, I found it terrifying to say the very least, when a bright light from a powerful torch shone in my eyes completely dazzling my vision. I did not know how to react in the circumstances and probably did what was natural in such an occasion; I froze. Quite mistakenly I thought it to be a raid and expected the very worst, I was totally mistaken, for instead of disaster, it was a group of local pastors led by Joel; who had come to take me out for dinner. *"But I thought you had no foo*d?*"* I asked.

"Come and see."

With their help and the bright light I quickly dressed, feeling slightly embarrassed at the mess of scattered clothes in my room, which of course had been totally due to the lack of light.

With the brilliant illumination now provided, I perfectly negotiated the damaged staircase we descended; and within a few minutes I found myself on the street outside.

"Come on and see this," Pastor Joel said.

We walked for a comparatively short distance until we arrived at the large city railway terminus station. Leading up to the platform I could see a large number of arches supporting the railway track. I was completely amazed for all I observed outside the arches were huge black cauldrons resting upon huge burning wood fires.

Hundreds of people were milling around them, so many that it was impossible to count them, or even hazard a guess. What I did notice though was that virtually every person that I could see appeared to be holding some form of a dish their hand.

Once my eyes got accustomed to the illuminated, paraffin lit, wooden torches I could see that long queues had formed in front of the pots, and a group of church leaders, which I shall refer to as the pastoral 'Cooks'. These faithful workers were dishing out great dollops of freshly cooked prawns to every person before them, it was sad to see that most of the recipients wore threadbare clothes and the little children were dressed in the strangely familiar sacking.

Even as I was standing there, I saw a great number of fishermen arriving holding large buckets, which were full to overflowing, with the tasty sea creatures.

It was my turn to eat, and I was ushered into the first archway where an *'oil drum'* had been utilised and had now become an improvised table; around it, several smaller drums which I could see had been placed there for our seating, three of the pastors now joined me, and although we did not speak the same language it was completely obvious by their mannerisms they were praising God for the bountiful harvest.

We were to be served, with what I consider to have been the best prawns I have ever tasted in my lifetime in an exquisite, improvised railway restaurant complete with lanterns of shimmering light. Even the strong smells contained in our prefabricated dining room had become insignificant and unnoticeable.

I now knew why the phone calls I had received on ZBC asking for Beira prawns had been made. God had answered the prayers pastor Joel had made and there was enough food for the whole city; talk about the feeding of the five thousand.

*

The next day I visited the hospital with an update on the work that had so far been completed.

Matilda was thrilled with what had been taking place, but with the present situation including the increasing numbers of people with waterborne diseases she was naturally somewhat restrained in her manner; *"Alan, would you come to our flat for a meal tonight?"*

I accepted and after a difficult time working in the church house, I was glad to return to the hospital with the short walk to the matron's house, it was a lovely flat but once again showed the signs of poverty and a reflection of what was taking place within the country, for with an acute lack of fuel along with every other amenity, it meant they had raised part of the wood block floor, and were burning it on the fire to cook whatever food they could find.

The meal was delicious; and I was offered a second helping, I was so glad that I refused for when we had eaten, Matilda's husband said that this meal had been their last food. *(After explaining their situation the Missionary House sent them food the very next day.)*

I was more than touched when Matilda and her husband Louis gave me a present, a small but beautifully made vase, carved out of a very expensive wood and at that time prohibited for export. Matilda's husband was a customs officer and wrote a note so that the present was not confiscated when I left the country; to this day it is in my office.

The rest of my time before returning to Zimbabwe was spent between the Missionary House and the hospital, with the hospital being the most important in my eyes. By the time I was due to leave the country the house was fifty per cent finished and the hospital well on the way to completion.

*

I was not sorry to get back to my flat and some type of normal living for a while, expecting to enjoy my decent cup of Zimbabwean tea. No chance, for my house girl had managed to pay her daughters school fees, but failed to pay the electric bill and my supply was cut off!!!!

CHAPTER 9

One again it was school holidays in the UK and after what seemed an age, Lil had flown out from London to join me in Harare. Timing had once again been perfect, for after I had driven her to our flat, and received the home news, I had the opportunity to update her on the situation here in Zimbabwe.

A little later in the day I looked into my office and whilst I was there, I found I had received a fax from Matilda at Beira Hospital. It was to say that the work on the building was virtually complete and should be ready for me to install the water purification plants within the next few days, finishing with three short words, *'Please come soon'*.

The message was poignant and written in such a manner that I knew she was extremely excited in the knowledge that it would save thousands of lives, but also reading between the lines I guessed it would be natural for her to be impatient for the completion of the life-giving work; knowing the absolute desperation for pure water in her hospital, I had no doubts about her deep concern.

Through previous visits, Harare was very familiar to Lil and with the increased shortages in the shops, she found the monotony of window shopping extremely boring, especially as most of the items we both liked were banned from export, certainly with little or no housework to do she found it difficult to occupy the hours whilst I was at work.

The lack of work was due to our hard-working housemaid, who expected Lil to let her into the flat the moment I left for work. This was at 06.00 a.m. each morning except for Sundays. Lil would then go out to town as soon as the shops opened. I felt sure that she probably knew the contents of nearly every department store in the city.

I shared the news of Matilda's fax with Lil when I got home, then dropped the bombshell by asking her if she would like to go to Mozambique with me?

Before giving her time to respond, I explained that our visit would be in two stages, the first phase would be to go to Mutare in the eastern highlands; on a routine visit where I could check the renal ward to see if all was running well, then after a couple of days using a borrowed car from the 'One Way Christian Centre', we could motor down the Beira corridor to the City Hospital for the final inauguration of the new water system.

She readily agreed, but raised only on one condition, this being that we should call at the orange farm, which she had heard so much about from me. She had specifically decided on her return, to bring some children's uniforms from the Epiphany School near to our church in the UK, these had been donated specifically for our work. Now with the perfect opportunity at hand, the visit to the orphanage would be an ideal time to take them.

Lil had visited Mutare previously, on several occasions, including the time when I was working in the cottage hospital and Mr Kitcat the Surgeon had removed a growth the size of a small egg from my head.

We were booked for dinner in the evening at a nice hotel; feeling somewhat embarrassed with the huge bandage on my scalp that covered the wound we arrived at the pre-booked time; Immediately the receptionist forbade me to go into the restaurant; the reason, not the bandage but, I had forgotten to bring a tie, Zimbabwe was still very formal and colonial in its ways. I did get away with it by borrowing a waiters tie. Neither of us had any doubts regarding the beauty of this small city.

I will always remember this trip, for being a railway enthusiast I had never travelled on the NRZ[2] to this part of the country before.

I have to admit to being quite eager to catch the comfortable overnight passenger train to our destination. I booked our tickets and paid for our sleeper, not forgetting the bedding that I had once forgotten on a far longer journey to Bulawayo. This only happened on one occasion, for after the uncomfortable nights journey that I endured I had sworn to myself, never again. During my stay in Zimbabwe I had

---

[2] National Railways of Zimbabwe

regularly travelled on the main line to Bulawayo.

This train was due to leave Harare at 2.00 p.m. in the afternoon. It was the scheduled sleeper, and from the timetable I knew it should arrive in Mutare at 06.30 a.m. the next day. How a journey of barely 200 miles should take that time I found incredulous, the road would have taken only three and a half hours, still with no car that I could trust on the main road (*even cycles could overtake me at times with the yellow peril*) and every scheduled Express coach booked for the next week, I was very pleased to catch the train. My friends at the General Hospital in Mutare had arranged for an ambulance to pick us up at the station.

After completing my work at the Central Hospital in Harare late in the morning on the day of departure, I drove home and picked up Lil who had carefully packed our baggage.

We had no telephone so Surei our house girl summoned a taxi from the nearby 'Avondale' shopping centre. It was only a stone throw from our apartment and the taxi arrived within five minutes, with Surei on board. Our transport got us to the station within fifteen minutes.

It was with no difficulty whatsoever, that we managed to find our booked apartment on the huge glass display board on platform 1, then collecting our bedding from a trolley, which had been placed nearby.

*

We settled into the small compartment and I set about finding out if there was a refreshment car on the train; with some disappointment I discovered there wasn't: but Lil had taken no chances and had at least been prepared, she had sensibly brought a good selection of food and drink for us.

So unlike the trains of the past, when you could purchase a lovely steak in the restaurant car, we had our own food to eat.

As was so typical of the fast-deteriorating railway system, our train started late; in fact very late, for it was not until 4.30 p.m. in the afternoon that we eventually pulled out of the station. Less than five minutes later, we came to an abrupt halt, and after an interminable length of time, I became bored, and poked my head out of the window of our compartment. I spent the next hour or so, watching a steady procession of pale skinned ants as they headed for a high termite nest some twenty foot from the train; it was totally fascinating to observe the assortment of items they carried, from small sticks and leaves to dead stag beetles all larger than themselves. Looking down at my watch, I was amazed when I saw the time, in fact my eyes ached and I knew I had been absorbed in watching the creatures far too long. Lil had finished her novel, and we both decided to a have a snack. The room was a bit cramped and for our own comfort we decided to take to our berths. These old-fashioned carriages had quite comfortable beds and I slept in the top bunk whilst Lil had the lower one, and after a good read I fell into a good sleep.

Daylight came quite early in the morning and being an early riser I woke at 5.30 a.m., I carefully, so as not to disturb my wife, climbed down till I stood on the carriage floor, we were at a standstill, and the termite nest was still in the same place, whilst the ants were still walking the dusty path, only this time empty handed and heading in the opposite direction.

I ascertained from the guard that, *"A goods van had been derailed yesterday 'Morning' and the steam crane did not arrive until four o'clock this morning. We should be leaving any time now."* I could almost hear him saying under his breath, *"I hope so."*

As if to confirm his statement, and within three minutes of him issuing it, there was a large judder as slowly and with a loud squeaking of rusty axles we were on our way.

It was a fairly uneventful ride and I was glad to arrive in Mutare only six hours late. No transport so I took a taxi to the pretty City Hospital to be greeted by the staff; that night we stayed in the city and in the morning went to the 'One Way Centre' to pick up the car.

The brother who was in charge during that period owned a garage and I remember so well that as he gave me his nearly new Peugeot 205. I still remember his earnest plea to be very careful with it! No wonder for transport was both expensive and difficult to come by.

Early in the morning we set off down the corridor, only stopping for a short comfort break in Chinoio where for the first time my wife saw the absolute poverty of the local people, I had to restrain her giving away all the clothes and good things we had with us for the orange farm.

This was her first taste of seeing legless children maimed for life by the lethal land mines and numerous ambushes carried out by the bandits.

We safely arrived at the orange farm by the track, certainly not using the short cut as I did on my previous visit. Trish showed Lil around and introduced us to some of the little children; one little girl effected Lil very much, her name was Precious, and at five years old she was totally traumatised. Unable to speak through seeing her parents and Grandparents massacred, plus when captured the 'bandits' had cut off her fingers.

We have never forgotten that little girl along with the other children who had found refuge in the farm. We had a long way to go still, so making a quick get-away we provisionally promised to call in on our return journey.

We passed the 400km. long Punge river and saw the results of the recent heavy rains and cyclones on the grass roundels, the homes of hundreds of locals submerged, up to their roofs in the floods, many people were still seated on the roofs with varying looks of despair, how long they had been waiting for rescue I could not tell; not only had they lost their homes, apart from that they had been starving. Now they had lost their only food supply; for the paddy fields that surrounded their homes had just ripened and were ready for harvest; now everything had been destroyed by the typhoon.

I was sad for them but after experiencing so many answers to prayer over the past year or so; I still believed that God understands and can answer in His own divine way. On our arrival at Beira I was once again subjected to the overwhelming faith of the Mozambique Christians. Joel invited us to pray with them following this dreadful disaster. We called in at the prayer meeting before going on to the missionary doctors house, sadly only staying for a short time as our host was expecting us.

The fervent prayers of the dozen or so Christians that met together, fired my faith. I knew they were starving yet somehow they managed to pray for the country and rulers first, then everybody else, also for every situation within the country, until finally they asked God for food, afterwards I learnt this was no ordinary prayer meeting but so anointed by the Holy

Spirit that it had continued all night long, with the results being that dozens of lorries filled with rice and grain arrived the very next day, supplying more than that which was lost.

We met the American missionaries who occupied a property which was owned by 'Siemens', the vast electronic company, and were warmly welcomed; I will always remember the 'water bed' in our room; fact it was the first time I had ever seen one, and was afraid I might drown in it. One thing I learned, the Americans look after their own and apart from a decent water supply they had every mod-con; The swimming pool was useful for it acted as a reservoir; we were given a few dollars by our host and this enabled us to use the shop which was intended only for the small American population; the dozen or so cans of Coca Cola we bought only remained with us for a few minutes, in fact less than fifty metres of the shop, as Lil showed her natural compassion towards a group of sparsely dressed children who followed us begging for a drink.

She was certainly disappointed when she saw the condition of the seafront house that was being renovated, and totally agreed with Tom the Welsh bricklayer who I wrote about on my previous visit; he was still continuing to say, *"Unscriptural to build your house upon the sand."*

The next day we went to the hospital and we were both amazed at the excellent work carried out by the builders; the next two days were hard work yet so worthwhile.

The first evening we ventured into the Indian ocean; I had not learnt to swim at that time but enjoyed the warmth of the water; no baths or showers were available, at either the doctors, or here at the Missionary House, so it was not only enjoyable but also refreshing, three of us ventured into the water, my wife and Michael from the house. Lil and Mike were swimming, unfortunately I was only paddling but the breakers were so impressive. I turned to speak to my wife and wondered where she was; I saw immediately that a powerful wave had knocked her over, and the sheer force of the receding current was keeping her face down on the gravel beneath the water, without the pair of us using our full strength she would have been drowned that very night. God protected us both from personal disaster.

The next day we spent at the hospital fitting the equipment and by evening we were ready to commission and present the hospital with enough pure water each day for up to 2,000 patients.

Morning came and at 10,00 a.m. the new system was due to be dedicated, I had been given the privilege of turning on the new supply. Lil reminds me of the long queue of people that stretched as far as we could see. Matilda was there, all the city dignitaries and now the answer to their prayers.

I switched on the power; and immediately I heard the pump start up; a lot of spluttering took place; causing me to feel something might be wrong, it wasn't and within seconds the tap used by the hospital staff and the families collecting water for the patients suddenly burst into life, the flow was so fast that its impact drenched those standing around; the response from everybody was jubilant to say the least, dancing, singing at the first pure water they had seen for a long time, the celebration went on for hours and the joy was complete.

On our return we made the promised stop at the orphanage and learned a lot more about their vision; God blessed us and Roy asked me some technical questions about their water supply, the path we took was quite interesting; for on either side of the track the thick elephant grass towered above us. I remarked to Roy about it, and his comment didn't help. "*Yes perfect for the bandits to hide in; that's how they caught us last time*!" I responded with a question, *"How do you know they are not in the grass now?"*

His reply, *"We don't know but we believe that God will take care of us*." Thankfully, we came to their well and pump and I was able to put their mind at ease by telling them that all was working well.

Their mind might have been at ease, mine wasn't, for apart from my nervousness in being captured by the bandits, I had just looked at my watch and realised we had a further eighty miles to go along the treacherous highway, before we reached the border near Mutare. And I knew for a fact that in slightly over one hour the border would be closed, stranding us an alien environment with all its dangers.

The suspension of the car must have been extremely strong, for the constant pounding and the occasional error as I caught the edge of a 'pot hole' must have taken its toll on the vehicle. It certainly took every ounce of concentration I could produce, for if we did not reach the border in time, we would have to sleep in the car. Apart from the uncomfortable claustrophobic feeling in the vehicle, it was inviting the bandits to capture us. To say I did not feel nervous would have been a gross understatement.

We arrived five minutes before the gate was due to be closed, and on our arrival found them partially closing it; the officials completely chose to ignore us, that was until I sounded my horn and kept my hand on the button. Eventually the two officials closing the gate turned in my direction, immediately I held my hand up and tapped the dial of my wrist watch, the time displayed still showed three minutes to go; my action acted like a red rag to a bull, they re-opened the gate and I entered the customs compound, the reticence of the officials was made even more obvious, when they refused to accept my papers of residency even though it was signed personally by Mr Robert Gabriel Mugabe the Prime Minister, *"The airports might take them, we don't."*

Lil was allowed through with no difficulties raised whatsoever, as she had her British passport; but my entry was far more questionable; for at that time I had no passport due to it having been stolen, the robbery took place whilst I was asleep, in fact during a long bus ride to Mutare some six weeks earlier. I had contacted the British High Commission and was waiting upon them to provide me with a duplicate, as is usual they had been extremely slow, so my residency papers were my only proof of identity.

The delay at the border turned out to a subterfuge, almost a form of mild blackmail for the customs officer in question had missed his transport home, and only agreed to let me through the border if I gave him a lift home.

The lift completed, the car returned and we had a pleasant night in Mutare, before talking a coach back to our flat in Harare. Mission completed.

CHAPTER 10

On my return to Zimbabwe I had a huge backlog of work to catch up on, and during my heavy schedule I once again had to visit Mpilo Hospital in the beautiful city of Bulawayo. I was surprised to see the large amount of traffic in what was to become my favourite town and future work place.

I was introduced to the Chief Technologist of Matabeleland hospital laboratories, Mr. Abel Waldman and we became good friends, a friendship that has lasted right up until the present time.

He was building a house outside the city at an area called Waterside; and the future property was situated down a rough track entitled Gary Owen Way; I never did discover whom Gary Owen was but I was privileged to help Abel over many years, both in the hospital setting and in his private life, oftentimes being a shoulder 'to cry upon' for the pair of us.

In the first instance, and outside of my hospital duties; he took me to the plot of land he had purchased, and showed me the basic layout of the footings for the bungalow; He needed me to find an underground well; prior to the city supply being installed on the building site to help the builders in their work.

It was a long time since I had cause to find a water source and I used a natural skill that my grandfather had first taught me as a teenager, this was using copper welding rods; it worked perfectly, for it did not take very long before the copper sticks demonstrated a circular motion above the source of the new supply; much to Abel's delight.

The next major project had been designing the sewerage system; the 'long drop' toilet on site was useful, but not very practical when shared with a multiplicity of biting flying objects, and several reptiles that frightened me to death.

Whilst fitting in regular visits to the building site during my work in the local hospital. Little did I know that this bungalow was going to be my God-given base for Rivers of Living Water in Zimbabwe for way over 20 years?

Abel held such a high position within the Matabeleland Public Health Services, that he had managed to organize a government facility of importation and Mpilo hospital became the main importers of aid from Rivers of Living Water, with the bungalow becoming a storage facility for me to distribute the God-given donations supplied by the charity. The house also provided me with secure accommodation, and kept my own personal bedroom, whenever I required it.

After setting up the Mpilo Hospital Kidney Unit I needed

to catch up on my work in Harare so I returned to my flat and back to my hospital work in the city.

It was quite apparent when things in Zimbabwe began to get difficult. My friends had a good nickname for me 'disaster', for I was on call from every direction, with shortages of equipment and many of the life-giving necessity's to help so many dangerously sick patients at the hospital, I could never be one hundred per cent certain of what was going to take place next.

Every hospital that I had worked in, needed different forms of help (oftentimes out of my normal remit and knowledge), yet quite early on in my work I met with a number of problems not of my own making (*except with the odd exception or two, you will read about one of these a little further on in this chapter*). One incident that sticks in my mind was regarding an import of artificial membranes. The importance for keeping the patients alive, made the delivery imperative and I had ordered from the UK for prompt delivery.

I was notified by FAX, that this important order had been sent immediately by air from the UK, as the manufacturers knew that it was crucial. On hearing the news, I hoped that we should receive the dispatched life protecting membranes as soon as was possible. They were necessary just to keep the ward functioning and continuing dialysing the kidney patients.

It was Friday afternoon and the renal department of Parirenyatwa hospital in Central Harare had phoned me to say that the shipment had arrived; immediately I set off from my flat to drive to the city customs house. I made sure that I was armed with my official requisition book, only to be rudely received on my arrival by a liveried young lady who immediately declared she did not trust me, and would have me arrested, I could tell she was deadly serious and immediately had to conceive some sort of plan in my head.

Mr Mugabe and Mr Moyo (the present Minister of Health in 2020) who could vouch for me were both out of the country for that weekend and I realized the seriousness of being detained by the customs. So taking no chances, I literally bolted and headed for the only place I considered I would be safe, or so I thought, this was the city office of the British High Commission.

After climbing the stairs I pushed open the door of the department and found myself facing a stereotype civil servant, who was seated at the reception desk, thankfully I was the only visitor, which meant I was alone with this petty bureaucrat.

Instantly his supercilious, and extremely bumptious attitude took the wind out of my sails, certainly as he failed to listen to my story and recognise the acute danger I could be in, *"Come back on Monday,"* had been his only words.

I strongly objected. Telling him politely, but firmly that his reply was tantamount to my abandonment.

"We have a garden party to prepare, for the ambassador." Then far louder; *"I repeat come back Monday or I will get security to remove you."*

Digging in my heels, I flatly refused to leave the building without some promise of help; in knowing my whereabouts for the next forty-eight hours.

The venom in the man's words as he virtually spat them out through his teeth; was full of malice as he rudely ordered two of his security guards to, *"Throw this idiot out,"* this whole episode left me dumbfounded, and the minders quite roughly assisted me in leaving the building immediately.

I still had visions of being arrested for committing no crime whatsoever and knew the conditions of those kept in custody.

One of the reasons behind this fear, had been a young Christian man who I had come to know in Harare named Gary he was quite troubled in his mind and suffered badly from epileptic fits, we prayed for him regularly and he would call at my flat for counselling. One day I had a call from Pastor John at Eastlea Assemblies of God Church to say Gary had been arrested and could I help. Working for State House had its advantages and I visited Central Police station to see what had happened. Evidently he had collapsed in the street and through his condition had frothed at the mouth, whilst his arms and legs had flayed in every direction, and through ignorance and fear on the part of the young police officers he had been arrested. Eventually he was handcuffed and detained, and the charge was demon possession. I arranged a warrant from State House that allowed me to visit him and I was shocked to see his ankles chained to a large iron ring in the floor. He was distraught and sadly all I could do was pray for him and talk to his guards, then arrange for him to join his sister on his release.

In my circumstances as far as this import was concerned, I had nobody to speak for me so quite possibly I would be arrested and put into one of the grey police cars, then taken to the nearest jail and locked away unknown by anyone, let alone by the representative of my own government.

Thinking back to Mozambique, it was not surprising that

the kidnapped British octogenarian who we had heard about at the orange farm who had been in captivity for six months, had only been released through the Danish authorities, and not her own by her own diplomats.

Feeling psychologically bruised after my visit to the embassy, and most certainly after the final altercation with the heavies, I speedily decided my next port of call would have be to the nearest foreign embassy to where I was situated at that moment, irrespective of country; this turned out to be the nearby Chinese legation.

Following the high-handed attitude of my visit to the British high commission I was received with open arms and the polite official behind the desk, listened intently to my story. At the end of my deliberation she disappeared into a nearby office.

After a short conflab behind closed doors, which I assumed would be with her superiors, a smartly suited woman emerged, holding out her hand in a gesture of goodwill; looking at the portrait which was hanging next to the predetermined portrait of Robert Mugabe, I recognized her as the Chinese Ambassador. She could not do enough for me; even to supplying one of their own agents to watch over me for the weekend. She even went the extra mile, by adding, "In fact up until Mr Mugabe returns if you wish?" They did, and on Mr Moyo's return I safely picked up the life-giving membranes.

God protected me but opened my eyes not to expect any protection from my own country should I need it in the future.

Through Abel's contacts and using hospital transport we travelled a few thousand kilometres looking at special needs and problems in the water supplies used by clinics.

This encounter with the British High commission was not to be my last, as one morning in early March I surprisingly received a large handwritten white letter addressed to me, which had a formal red wax seal upon its flap.

It turned out to be an invitation for Lil and myself to attend a reception hosted by the Ghana High Commission to celebrate the anniversary of Ghana's independence. The ambassador asked us if we could take him and his two 'ladies' in my Ford Anglia car in a ceremonial procession through the main street, Samora Machel.

We had become friends and he lived in our block of flats, I have to admit to being deeply concerned when he requested to use my transport. Taking it for granted that his country's finances were very low and they could not even find a Mercedes to use.

We loaded up with the Gambian ambassador and his two ladies; with difficulty they squeezed into the back of the car, Lil sat in the front with me. The colourful costumes that the three of them wore put me to shame yet both Lil and I looked smart in our best western European clothes.

I painfully remember with a great deal of embarrassment that with a smoke screen that blocked the vision of the following entourage of transport the '*Yellow perils*' engine cut out at least four times during the procession and needed a fair bit of coaxing to start, the large number of posh Mercedes and the few Rolls that were behind me in the motorcade were forced to wait whilst the well-wishers on the edge of the road kindly pushed my ancient vehicle enabling the car to continue.

All would have been well if, on our ignominious arrival at the recently built Sheraton Hotel, my car had not decided to shed its sump oil on the new yellow brick forecourt outside the main entrance as I discharged the ambassador.

The assortment of flunkeys and cleaners that pushed my car to the nearest parking place away from view, whilst they scrubbed the newly laid stones clean of the oily mess.

It was very noticeable that the large number of smartly dressed diplomatic staff along with their relevant ambassadors were lined up to greet us; politely shaking the hand of our friend; until we came to the British legation, who promptly turned their backs on us; no doubt embarrassed when they remembered the plea I had made for protection.

We were quite embarrassed when we entered the assembly room with no seats being available; standing before a long table filled with magnificent golden tureens we could not help being amazed at the quality of the food, which had been laid out decoratively upon the flower-strewn tables.

Who should come to our rescue? None other than the Chinese ambassador once again, who having remembered our previous meeting had made us more than welcome to join them on her table.

I remember following this totally unnecessary rudeness by the commission. I composed a polite, yet extremely straight letter to Mrs Thatcher who was Prime Minster in the UK at that time about both incidents.

The time had come for my return to the UK. The Rev Nelson Bainbridge, the local Moderator in the URC (Equivalent of a Bishop), cajoled me in the nicest possible way to becoming an ordained minister in the United Reformed Church; I had my credentials by this time in the Assemblies of God Zimbabwe, but spending more time in the Bournemouth area, and with some serious problems within the church at Throop near Bournemouth, he felt that I should officially train to become a Minister; we both prayed and I went for an interview in Church House at Southampton. The committee talked for hours before accepting me; and Nelson kept coming out to me to say all would be well; eventually I was given the offer of training for three years on a part time basis at The Anglican Training School, at Bath and Wells Theological College in the close at Salisbury Cathedral; although unofficially I was running the Throop URC church in Bournemouth; keeping up with tutorials; and running a water treatment business of my own for our income. Plus going over to Zimbabwe for a couple of months every year. Talk about juggling and keeping everything moving forward. It was challenging to say the least; we moved into the manse and after my wife and church members worked hard in decorating the badly rundown property for weeks on end; stayed in the large house for twenty years, during which time we worked tirelessly, especially Lil my wife, in holding together a loving and kindly fellowship with a very large junior church. God blessed my time in Throop and through the United Reformed Churches in our region and our own church members enabled me to collect and plan for the difficult days that lay ahead for the folks in Zimbabwe.

We had numerous blessings, which would fill a book, but inevitably it became God's time for us to go, I became seventy years old and the moderator felt the time had come for me to retire. Sadly, the church was then closed down, and after a great deal of prayer, I took up the God given pastorate of Rossmore Gospel Church in Parkstone in Poole Dorset;

strangely I had spoken in that little hall last when I was seventeen years of age. But yet again we have both been blessed in the pastorate for the last ten years, and Peter Orton a Bible-trained believer, a much younger man than me has recently joined me as co-pastor.

Just before returning home from Zimbabwe I feel I should share with you about one of the '*man made*' disasters that I spoke about, and particularly participated in; one that I will now tell you, was certainly of my own making, Joice my final house girl lived in the front room of a fairly modern bungalow and she was unable to cook her Sunday Lunch for the family, *"Boss the electric has gone out and I can't feed the family, can you help?"* Within fifteen minutes I had turned up at the house with my small bag of tools, to be greeted ecstatically by the young woman and a host of children.

The fuse box was very old fashioned and unfortunately no fuse wire was available so with great improvisation, (*or so I thought at the time and taking my life into my hands*) I removed the fuse holder and taking a small but quite long nail I folded it to fit into the slots that the fuse holder normally slipped into. Delicately I turned it on and Joice informed me that her sockets were now working. I congratulated myself on my innovation. That was until she turned on the stove. The noise at the rear of the bungalow was enormous and everything run by electricity ceased to work; gingerly walking around the house I came to the outhouse in which the fuse box had been fitted, had being the operative word, for the fuse box was now in the middle of the unkempt garden and a large hole had appeared in the wall. I guess the council who owned the house, were not amused.

The meals for the family were cooked at my flat and on the Monday Joice moved out to new lodgings with her family.

During the next two years God was teaching me to serve Him in a very special way, this certainly including building bridges between myself and the people of Zimbabwe for a future that at that time I could never have envisaged.

CHAPTER 11

Monde School

Reverend Betty Williams was a United Reformed Church minister in the village of Lytchett Minster near Poole in Dorset. In the late 1980s Betty and her husband Basil had taken a holiday in Zimbabwe, staying at the small city of Victoria Falls.

Whilst on holiday, Betty had been drawn to an advertisement for one of the many sightseeing trips that were arranged by the tourist board to introduce foreign visitors to the local villages; this one in particular was to a fairly spaced out settlement called *Monde*. Having whet her appetite the pair of them decided to take this excursion and on the journey Betty was captivated by the long line of both women and children walking the long dusty road to the village with an assortment of heavy water containers balanced upon their heads, their straight backs indicated that this exercise must have been carried out many times over a long period she immediately asked the guide where they had come from.

He replied, "*The village water supply has dried up and the woman and the children have to walk twelve kilometres, (over seven miles) twice a day.*"

"*Why no men?*" Basil asked.

"*Traditionally it's a women's job.*" No further information was volunteered, and they noticed the majority of the men sitting outside their huts, '*resting.*'

Neither Betty nor Basil could get this out of their minds and when later in the trip they were introduced to the village chief, Basil asked about the question of fresh water for the villagers? This persuasive man had no difficulty in urging them to collect money for a water project that could extract Potable (*Pure*) water from the deep, badly contaminated now disused wells within the community.

Returning home to the UK and collecting quite a large sum of money towards the project they were faced with the dilemma of what to do about the work?

The couple knew of my knowledge and involvement regarding water treatment in Zimbabwe and Betty asked if I could visit the village when I was next in the Victoria Falls area, to check and make sure the gifts which they had sent to the village had arrived, then could I design a suitable pumped water supply for the Chief's village, she also asked if I might distribute the generous donations to the villagers and to the local primary school which they had collected.

Sadly, we never saw these gifts, for the Chief was a rogue and after my visit disappeared with their generous donations and the last I heard was that the police were still trying to catch him for a number of different crimes; not doubt from other 'tourists'.

Even through this setback, God showed me quite practically then, and on reflection over many years that he had a perfect plan by using the situation to open the door for a far greater opportunity in their community for many years to come.

In fact Monde primary school has required a greater amount of help over the years than I could ever have imagined, and for me has proved to be a great blessing within my regular yearly visits.

During my last few years of working in a number of hospital renal units for the Zimbabwe Health Service I had attended a number of compulsory, and very interesting courses at Parirenyatwa Hospital, one of which had been based on the *'new'* killer bug called *'aids.'*

On visiting this forgotten village, I soon discovered that by far the majority of children at this large school had lost their parents through this Aids epidemic. Regrettably, this had been exacerbated because most of the men had through poverty, been forced to work away from home for long periods of time. At that time prostitution was rife and through their promiscuity they introduced this dreadful disease.

The kind hearted masters at the school encouraged by their dedicated headteacher were looking after the children like surrogate parents, certainly an extremely generous gesture on the part of the teachers, as at that time in the countries deepening financial crisis teachers, like many other public sector workers, were only getting their wages spasmodically.

Receiving pay packets that were few and far between, made life very difficult for the vast majority of government workers. Even in my own case, and after missing only one month's salary, I remember making the decision, that each month on pay day I would go to the huge Government pay office in Harare and wait all day if necessary outside the paymaster's office for my monthly cheque. In fact I made it clear to the staff that I would not leave the building until I was paid my wage. Eventually I was paid, notably five minutes after the banks had closed their doors for the night!!!

Another problem for the headteacher was the fact that there had been no fees collected from at least 90% of the children attending the school. Officially the children should have been sent home for not paying; not at Monde School, and only through the caring headteacher, and her persuasive technique the whole school had developed into a community, even though she had been called to Hwange, the provincial education headquarters of Matabeleland and received severe castigations for her 'inadequacies'; in obtaining the fees.

During the next fifteen years we were able to help considerably in supplying pens paper, medicines such as paracetamol and wound dressings, even sweets supplied by Throop Junior Church children and later by the children at Rossmore; also school uniforms donated by local parents for many of the children.

Following a news item on our local ITV channel, I received a call asking if I wanted help at the school, this was by the owner of an engineering firm. The gentleman had a son attending Canford Public School in the Wimborne area of Dorset and he wanted to introduce the lad to an African experience.

At his own expense he financed a trip to Monde and apart from doing the magnificent job of repairing the defunct water pump; they then managed to set up a large vegetable garden to teach the children of the school how to grow their own food. Also this would act as back up for being unable to buy vegetables from a supplier.

He spent some time there and it proved a real blessing to the school, in fact through my yearly visits, I am certain the gardens still remain to this day.

As I write this episode of my story, one particular and extremely memorable visit to the school with Abel comes to mind.

During the late nineteen eighties, and well into the nineteen nineties the BBC and Bournemouth *Daily Echo* had given a very fair coverage of my work in Africa, and had drawn the interest of a young BBC reporter named Steve; he wanted to see for himself what the situation was in Zimbabwe and asked if he self-funded could he join me?

In one way, it had been extremely hard for me to decide if it was the right step to take, For I had to weigh up the pros and cons of the situation and make the final difficult decision before taking him with me to Zimbabwe, certainly due to a strict ban on the BBC by the Zimbabwe Government. I had no doubt that if he was discovered as working for the banned corporation, then I would have lost my credibility and my opportunity of government support, perhaps even being refused entry to country in the future, this of course would stop the continuance of my work, also not be fair on my friend Abel as I lived and worked from his house.

On the Pro side, at least the young man would be supporting himself, for the BBC told him that they could not support him in any way thus in my opinion deeming him to be freelance; also he would truthfully be able to film the excess poverty and see for himself the acute difficulties many of the people faced daily. Hopefully, the news bulletin he was on would give the much-needed publicity for the work to continue.

After praying I agreed with caution that he could join me as my co-helper; providing he did not carry out any activity that could jeopardise our mission.

He was careful and even brought a typical home movie camera belonging to his girlfriend to film on.

One of the things he did was to attend Hatfield AOG and evidently for the first time in his life he was moved to tears as he saw the poverty-stricken members of the congregation praising and thanking God; sadly, he was so moved that he forgot to put the sound on the film he had made of their worship.

As happens on a regular a basis in all areas of Southern Africa and with the Monde area of Victoria Falls district being no exception, they had experienced an extended drought. We arrived in the village to find not only a lack of vegetables, but also the two hundred or so 'resident' pupils were without meat of any kind; the excited teachers told me of the latest news. A rogue elephant had run amok, beating down the huts and trampling on the people. Unfortunately, the poor beast had been shot and its meat, although I was told tasted quite obnoxious, was available to be purchased and could feed the children the school for up to a month.

Steve wanted to film the incident and after consulting with Abel we took the hospital truck for at least thirty kilometres over the rough terrain until we arrived within walking distance of the village, then taking a number of buckets, borrowed from the school we walked till we came upon a group of villagers, they were gathered round a very large mound of pink flesh, the butchered remains of the beast had been prepared for sale.

Abel negotiated a fair price and the reporter interviewed the village head for BBC news.

The faces of the children were a joy to see as they received their first decent meal for weeks, plus sweets to enjoy. It was like feeding the 5,000 and gladly plenty left over for the following week or two.

This episode had a slight repercussion for me, as on our return to the UK and shortly after the episode involving the elephant was shown, I received a call from the BBC, asking if I could receive a call from an irate viewer that they were unable to appease.

The icy tone of the caller left me in no doubt as to her stance, for her opening words lambasted me regarding the death of the elephant. *"Why did you allow them to kill the beautiful creature?"*

I gently explained about the animal destroying everything, and that it had to be destroyed; but at least its meat would save the children's lives. Her reaction was unexpected; *"I would rather see the children die than that poor beast."*

I thanked God, and firmly believed that we had been used

to buy and give them food enough for the next few weeks ahead.

Over the years I had attended a large number of clinics that had been suffering from cholera and installed water purification equipment to clean the badly neglected medical centres. I was taken ill on one of my attempts after clearing the disease from the water source. And will never forget the care I received from Abel and his mother as they nursed me through the dreadful symptoms associated with Cholera. I shall always be grateful for my friends over the years; Abel's mum is with the Lord now.

My God given vision plus His enabling power allowed me to supply safe water to the whole of Matabeleland public health laboratories, which in turn supplied the clinics.

Each day whilst I was in Zimbabwe, I experienced God's hand working, in fact far too many incidents and their solutions to write in this short book.

One miraculous experience I do remember so well, took place in the small town of Binga which is situated 192 miles north of Bulawayo and on the banks of the 220 kilometre long Lake Kariba.

In 2010 we visited this provincial district and I was introduced to the medical officer for health to the district; he was a local Pastor and took us to his church; which had recently been built. Water was again the problem and the health laboratory provided sufficient drinking water for the hospital, and outlying clinics. At least it should have, not in this case and it was necessary for me to spend a couple of days installing a water treatment plant in the laboratory. We stayed in a large, once thriving, (*in colonial days*) lodge on the lakeside. The main memory I have is that of the beautiful tiger fish meals that we enjoyed; Fish for breakfast; fish for lunch; fish for supper!!

Once our work was completed and the plant in operation we held a presentation ceremony which was more of a prayer and praise meeting, after which, we left for Victoria Falls Hospital where I had to restore the large purifier that we had donated some four years previously and was still widely used for a huge area around the Falls district.

The miracle took place exactly a year later when I was planning my itinerary.

Whilst I was engaged in my filter changing programme, and working in our base at Mpilo Hospital; I realised how big the work in this major hospital had become, considering I had installed eight water treatment plants in strategic points within the large hospital complex; these included two units large enough to supply over 2,000 gallons of pure water and with visitors carrying water vessels on bikes, motor scooters, and ambulances to every location within thirty miles of Bulawayo. The two largest machines had broken down and needed stripping, plus rebuilding and sterilizing immediately. I had barely completed the work when Abel said he felt we should go to Binga again. I was not happy as it was a long journey and we had enough work at Victoria Falls to keep us busy, I objected, "*They are quite capable of changing filters.*" Abel responded by saying he felt certain that we must go again.

I gave in and we started out very early in the morning, arriving at the provincial hospital about midday. The welcome we received was extraordinary and it did not take long to find out the reason; for the night previous to our visit, there had been a thunderstorm and a sheet of lightning had struck the machine and virtually destroyed it.

I always carried enough spares to rebuild the equipment and on this occasion renewed the equipment and left them with pure water.

They had not even used up their safety storage tanks before we had them in operation.

The joy shown and the prayer meeting held on the completion of my work by the hospital heads of department, demonstrated their thanks to God for answered prayer.

This was only one situation in so many where we knew God was working and over the years I had the joy of installing over 14 different machines in different parts of the country; and as with all equipment, and a constant change of itinerant workers I had to train new people virtually every year in basic maintenance.

CHAPTER 12

Part of dismantled water treatment plant for Victoria Falls

2019 was certainly one of the most challenging and memorable trips since my work for Rivers of Living Water in Zimbabwe had commenced in 1989. Once I had completed the work at Beira hospital our focal point had moved from Mozambique to Zimbabwe where I was still working.

The year I refer to was certainly problematic, in fact as far as I can remember; the most difficult in over 25 years, which even included the Beira period and although I could write about every year with its joys and difficulties I feel this final chapter of my book summarises to some degree all that took place during those years of serving God in Africa.

As had been usual, on every trip, I attempted to make my plans as precise as was possible, the reason behind this had been to make the best impact on the needs of the people, certainly in the later years with the limited time of just a few weeks, and of course equally important that I should not waste the charity's finances. On every trip there is always problems, some minor, some major with broken-down and unreported plants to repair, such as Binga in my last chapter.

Not only breakdowns but also transport problems, fuel shortages, occasional sicknesses, etc. However I can truly say God had directed me through every situation.

The plans I had made for my 2019 visit included not only carrying out general maintenance on a number of the 22 units (*To visit every site with the huge distances involved; would have been impossible*). But also knowing the logistics of the terrain and the importance to save lives from waterborne diseases I decided that the Falls were probably the most important, and an extremely needy area at that particular time. My decision was based on the greatest number of lives protected by putting in a larger water purification machine in Victoria Falls Hospital; the old machine had been temporarily repaired by myself the previous year and could no longer cope with the requirement of dozens of minor clinics that relied totally on the central hospital for pure water.

It had been reported to me whilst at home in the UK that a large number of Cholera patients were turning up daily at the hospital and they were desperate for pure water, I was so glad when eventually the time had arrived for Austin, my helper for the past two years and myself to leave for Africa.

Our plane arrived from Johannesburg and had landed safely on time; this was typical of my favourite airline South African Airways. I looked at my watch and saw it was just after one o'clock; very quickly I paid for our visas, and checked through customs prior to entering the baggage area of the newly built air terminal. A beautiful modern building situated about fourteen miles from the city of Bulawayo. For me, the baggage came through quite quickly and for the first time that I could remember; it had not been searched.

Stepping out into the terminal building, I was greeted once again by my faithful friend Abel Waldman; although I had hired a car, he was still anxious enough after so many years to make sure I had come safely through the formalities.

Not quite so straightforward as I had first thought, or at least not for Austin; for it took a good thirty minutes or so, whilst he and his baggage was being thoroughly inspected. Only when they were satisfied that he was not a smuggler did they allow him to leave the customs hall.

Both Abel and I gave an audible sigh of relief as he joined us.

After Abel greeted him it was agreed that Austin would travel in the hospital truck to his house, whilst I sorted out my hired car with Eurocar.

Being quite well known in Bulawayo with the hire company most formalities were skipped. However, the cursory search for dents and bumps on the car prior to hiring the vehicle, turned out to be a full-blown epic.

Once the twenty or so photographs of the damage had been taken, I drove their '*newest*' car along the main road to Abel's house on the outskirts of the city, where our accommodation would be once again, and where also the latest delivery from our shipment had been stored.

My patience has never been the best, and I have always detested wasting time; but when over an hour and a half had elapsed since I had first arrived at Abel's house in the Riverside area of Bulawayo and there was still no sign of him, I felt cause to be concerned.

I decided to drive to Mpilo Hospital and see if I had made a mistake and they were in Abel's office in the Public Health Laboratory. They weren't and talking to his staff I was told he had not been there since he left for the airport at midday.

I made up my mind to phone Pat, Abel's sister at her house in the Hillside area of Bulawayo. Thinking he might have taken Austin there for coffee as we had done so many times in the past.

Somewhat annoyingly she was not at home, so all I could do was to return to his house.

This whole episode of driving through the city gave me the opportunity to see just what was taking place in Bulawayo, and from what I could observe, there seemed to be a fair amount of police activity. I went through at least four road checks, unimpeded I have to say; but I also noticed a large number of military personnel arriving at a road junction near to the now disused Ascot racecourse and outside the Holiday Inn Hotel. They had trucks overflowing with scaffolding and barbed wire; I recognised the materials, for in past years they had been used for in the construction of roadblocks. A number of the soldiers were armed and I could see they carried Russian rifles.

I asked myself the obvious question. What was happening? Did they expect a riot? I could not fail to see the long queues of cars waiting for fuel. It was the same at every garage that I passed, some of these queues stretched for a mile or so. Reminding me of the past when I lived in Avondale.

Whilst I had been at the hospital I had picked up information from the laboratory staff, whom I knew very well, that they had heard very strong rumours of probable civil unrest, with the local city dwellers being joined by villagers that were coming into the city for a demonstration.

I was not surprised by this news, as with the severe hardships they were facing, mainly through the lack of fuel and excessive food prices, when food was available, along with acute shortages of healthcare. So after seeing the troops, I guessed this could well be part of a lockdown.

Back at Abel's bungalow the house girl was back from picking up her daughter from school and let me into the garden; where I waited a further sixty minutes before the pair of them turned up; *"I received a call from a relative, and took a little detour,"* Abel explained.

I should have guessed, so typical of my Zimbabwean friend I thought to myself.

After a few minutes, my frustrations had quelled; and not wishing to waste any further time I entered a room in the bungalow, which had been piled high with our equipment.

Sadly during the journey from the UK our shipment had been unloaded and left uncovered in the pouring rain at a Uganda airport and the blankets and medicines were sodden and filthy dirty.

Even when it was delivered Abel had to get enough fuel to get to Harare. This had been exceptionally difficult for him, certainly due to the lack of petrol and diesel with up to a two-week wait at a garage for a delivery. I sent him American dollars to purchase as much as he could buy on the black market. Once he had obtained petrol he managed to get enough to arrive at Harare on time; this enabled him to collect our recently cleared goods before extortionate charges were added. His problems continued as it took several days to get enough fuel to get home, during this time he was forced to sleep in his own vehicle along with the mosquitoes, in case the goods were stolen.

Needless to say through his grim determination and loyalty he brought everything in the shipment to his house for my inspection and eventual distribution.

I continued to rummage through the items and was amazed to see Abel's maid had washed and ironed every article!! Very little of that years shipment had been destroyed, a miracle in itself.

Victoria Falls has held some hilarious memories over the years, including quite a dangerous one. The particular situation that comes to my mind, from about twenty years ago, in fact in my early days of visiting the hospital; and being extremely ignorant about baboons, I had accidently left the hospital doors open. Within a few moments of entering the main corridor of the infirmary I heard a noise behind me, turning I immediately saw two of the vicious animals following me. I clapped my hands loudly and after showing their fanged teeth in anger, they bolted back into the garden outside; once they had left the building I watched the disgruntled beasts eyeing me up; then without warning, they ran to the unit I was working in; and without hesitating, one of them got hold of the stand pipe supplying the water supply to the garden, and yanked the tap off, immediately both animals ran a safe distance and turned to face me, one of them held the tap in his hand. (*I could have sworn it was laughing at me)* He then threw the heavy brass bibcock in my direction leaving the gushing water pipe with a gesture of defiance that could not be misinterpreted.

My first job at Victoria Falls provincial hospital that year was recoupling the new stopcock!!

No work is ever easy in Zimbabwe and trying to get plumbing materials is almost impossible, so when I travel I always take everything but the kitchen sink; Not the year of 2019, for the shortages of fuel made it impossible to take our car the 439 Kilometres *(273 miles)* from Bulawayo to Victoria falls or the opposite way another 440 Kilometres *(274 miles)* to Harare for my work at Falcon school.

In previous years I had been given government fuel vouchers and this enabled me to fill the tanks of the ancient, 300,000-kilometre Government Toyota mini bus, now not only did I not have use of the bus, but also no fuel for my car.

Whilst servicing the large number of purifiers at Mpilo Hospital, Bulawayo we had to go to a local store nearby for some parts. The shop was situated next to Barbourfields football stadium, I thought there was to have been a match in the near future, for there were literally hundreds of uniformed police, and for the first time in my life several army water cannon trucks outside, I thought the spectators must have been far rougher than I had ever seen there!! Once we had obtained our goods I forgot about them and continued with the task in hand.

After the official presentation I decided to make arrangements to go to two destinations, the first was Victoria Falls Hospital, whilst the second was to visit my old church in Harare and then deliver a pump for Falcon School near to

Harare; the school had been a project of Revd Wilbert Sayimani and his wife (sadly Irene went to be with the Lord since this chapter was written).

Wilbert is a Zimbabwean Minister pastoring a church in my own town of residence Bournemouth; we had arranged to stay at his bungalow in Waterfalls district of Harare; both Austin and myself were looking forward to this as the previous year we had been picking the most delicious mangoes from his lovely garden, In fact I had been quite pleased that whilst we were in the house, Irene, Wilbert's wife had taken us to the school and I had arranged for a pump to be delivered and to be fitted on my return trip.

Austin had been driving us back from the school when he felt the strain of the many Zimbabwe drivers, on the outskirts of the city I took over; and when back at her house she phoned Wilbert to update him, during the conversation I heard Irene telling him, that my driving was just like the Zimbabweans, I felt so pleased and felt it a compliment until Wilbert said that was not a complement!!! I guess my driving reflected the years I had spent in that locality.

This time there could be no driving outside of Bulawayo, so I brought bus tickets to Harare; these were dated a week later and after we had completed our local work, at the Falls.

To get to Vic Falls to install the new equipment was a different kettle of fish, the first being our mode of transport.

My first thought, had to be to travel by train, as the bus service was infrequent and unreliable. I attempted to book two sleepers, one for Austin the other for myself, only to be told that they did not accept any booking until it was time for the evening sleeper to leave, I had been told the same story when my son-in-law who had visited me in Zimbabwe a few years ago needed to get back to Harare for his flight home. It's not always what you know; but whom you know? For over thirty years I have been a constant visitor to Bulawayo railway museum and my leisure time is usually spent in the old station masters office with Gordon Murray the present curator and ex-employee of National Railways of Zimbabwe who had arranged Jonathan's passage several days before he had to leave.

Geordie came to the rescue once again and arranged for us to have booked seats as railway workers. He then gave me a railway workers hat as a present in case any questions were asked.

The equipment for the hospital was then dismantled and put into two large suitcases our clothes for two days were put into carrier bags.

The epic journey commenced with Suzanne Abel's Fiancé driving us to the station, where I paid for the tickets, the only thing cheap in Zimbabwe 1st class sleepers for £12.00 return!!!!

The carriage going to Vic Falls was not overcrowded and I slept well on a comfortable bed; unfortunately, Austin did not have the same comfortable bed as me but still enjoyed the trip.

We arrived at Vic Falls about two hours late, which in this case was quite good for NRZ as I have touched upon in a previous chapter.

There was only one taxi parked there. And as we had left by a side gate, we beat any other passenger that might have required it.

We hired it and the driver took us to the hospital; I am certain that under the circumstances that it had had been provided by God for he had no other business on; and I was able to arrange for him to pick us up and run us around as required.

I started work instantly as we were very limited in our time, so I reassembled the new equipment as quickly as I could, leaving it ready to install early the next morning.

It was nearing the end of the day, and we had to find our own accommodation for two nights, unlike in the past, the hospital no longer had the funds to pay for our accommodation.

The driver was summoned, and he took us to a number of places where we could stay within our budget. Eventually we found a lovely backpackers place where I booked us in for the two nights and I looked forward to our evening meal:

We picked up the menu and both ordered our evening meal from an extremely limited menu; *"Sorry boss we have no food,"* the familiar form of address that remained from colonial days greatly annoyed me, and with my usual response I politely explain I was not his boss; anyhow, apart from that, he appeared to be correct, for having led us to believe, no food was available.

The taxi found a takeaway and we purchased some food and brought it back to the room. I slept well which was most unusual for this sub-tropical area of Zimbabwe; I did not have one mosquito in my net that night.

The next morning surprisingly there was toast for breakfast, along with bacon and egg. I learnt that the chef had gone home early the previous night; *(hence the reason for no food).*

We called the taxi and went to the hospital. My training session started for Austin and the laboratory technicians as I commenced to install the new equipment. I was very wary in turning off the water to commence the work, as three years prior to this; I had missed being bitten by a baby snake curled around the leaking stop tap; this was thanks to a sharp-eyed lady technician, who screamed the place down.

The day was spent installing the equipment, and we left for our lodging place in our taxi. In the evening Austin joined me in the lounge and we watched Sky News from nearby Zambia. My blood ran cold when I saw the African headlines for it showed Bulawayo with the troops having taken over to stop riots that were taking place.

The next morning we arrived at the hospital to find it closed; the shops were also closed, so I decided to go to the station to make sure our bookings on the night sleeper were ok: The station was locked up but I could see the station master in her office; so putting on my railway hat I knocked the door; she was very friendly and genuinely told me not to worry she had been told there was a derailment just outside Bulawayo and the crane was on its way from Harare.

Unfortunately, we had to return to return to Bulawayo not only to catch the coach to Harare; but also to fly out to the UK, in just over a week's time. Our taxi driver took us back to our accommodation and I negotiated a further night's stay; that whole day was spent arranging transport back to Bulawayo, and it was frustrating discovering the area was on total lockdown, no shops open, in fact the majority had been boarded up to stop pilfering, no cafes, just a couple of takeaways.

The coach station was absolutely full of buses, but no drivers or managers.

I considered hitch-hiking, one or two cars were taking

passengers but I did not feel easy in my mind. Thankfully, we didn't take up the lift, for we heard the next day that the cars were attacked by vandals at the halfway hotel near to Hwange Game Park and stoned.

For two more days we were stuck, we missed the deadline for our coach to Harare. But at least the hospital re-opened and we could put the finishing touches to both purifiers; every few hours we visited the nearby coach station, and then finding no joy; our taxi driver took us to the station; but the station master said the sleepers would be reserved once they knew a train would arrive.

There is an airport at Victoria Falls so I called at the city offices of Air Zimbabwe to see if any flights were available; they were; but could only get me to Harare; and for the price of £800 each, totally out of the question.

We lived off of takeaway food during the day and the backpackers breakfast in the mornings.

On my final visit to the station three days later I was told a train had left Bulawayo and would arrive at Vic Falls during the afternoon; returning to Bulawayo overnight.

Needless to say once we had settled up for our accommodation; we took the taxi to the station and said goodbye to the excellent driver and our helper and friend of Austin's called Trust; we had visited his house and seen the meagre spread of food for him and his children that his wife had managed to get.

Each of them had a fish head and a few lettuce leaves on their plates, we were invited to join them, but unprepared to eat their food we took the taxi into town and purchased some large pizzas for the family.

The train came into the station, and with a blackening sky from a massive thunderstorm that was gathering we took our berths.

The train was full to overflowing yet the stationmaster had reserved us first class accommodation and after a few hours we left the station, with a packed lunch brought at OK supermarket, which had now re-opened.

The magnificent storm lasted for a good 80 Kilometres and both of us spent time in the corridor with countless others watching the lightning through the continuous downpour, eventually returning to our cabins and having a fairly restful sleep until we had safely arrived at Bulawayo station.

The main purpose of our visit was now completed and I knew that the Victoria Falls Hospital would be able to supply pure water to countless people for many years to come.

Hopefully until that beautiful country returns to its feet.

Back to Abel's and for the final week we had purchase some black-market petrol to enable us to service the final two hospitals in the area and return the car to the airport.

Looking back on this the last trip before I wrote this book, I realised the extent that God's hand had been upon my life over so many years.

For me it is a privilege to have started out my working life as a local plumber, never guessing what would take place throughout the years and as an encouragement to every reader give God the opportunity to teach, and use you in whatever way He chooses.

(Luke 9;58) *Jesus replied, "Foxes have holes and birds of the air have nests, but the Son of Man has nowhere to lay his head."*

(59) *He said to another man, "Follow me."*

But the man replied, "Lord, first let me go and bury my father."

(60) *Jesus said to him, "Let the dead bury their own dead, but you go and proclaim the kingdom of God."*

(61) *And another also said, "Lord, I will follow thee; but let me first go bid them farewell, which are at home at my house."*

(62) *Jesus replied, "No-one who puts his hand to the plough and looks back is fit for service in the kingdom of God."*

A FEW FACTS AND FIGURES

Alan Clarredge was born in 1940 at Poole Hospital in Dorset and brought up in the beautiful town of Wimborne. After leaving school at 15; he trained as a plumber for five years. Following his apprenticeship, Alan became a water inspector for Poole and East Dorset water board and was based at Okeford Fitzepaine in North Dorset.

In 1964 He married Lilian from Southampton and they had two children, Simon and Amanda, they purchased a house in Christchurch in Dorset and Alan took up a position in the works department of Bournemouth Corporation.

Alan was made redundant from local government and moved on to become a service engineer for Permutit water treatment, after a few years he became technical advisor to the company and was based at company headquarters in London; It was decided by Permutit's management that he should receive medical training in specialized water treatment for a new business venture. This was to be in the field of renal dialysis, which was at that time using a new process, which would require new equipment to purify the water for cleaning the blood during dialysis. He trained at Liverpool University Hospital; and ultimately become a technical advisor in the new field.

Eventually Alan left Permutit and became medical advisor to Culligan water treatment, advising them, and designing their international renal programmes.

He went to work in Zimbabwe in 1983 after being approached at a medical conference in Budapest by Mr Obadiah Moyo.

Obadiah was setting up a new water treatment plant in a small clinic in State House with the sole purpose of looking after President Mugabe's first wife Sally, who was suffering from acute renal failure. He had a much wider vision than the President's residence, and he had chosen Alan for a much larger operation than this clinic, so whilst he was carrying out his work at State House Alan was asked to install purification and kidney dialysis plants in five major hospitals within Zimbabwe, during this period Mr Moyo was studying hard to become a doctor. (*At the time this narrative was written Dr Moyo has become the Minister of Health for Zimbabwe*).

Alan carried out this work which has to be said was extremely difficult at times due to the acute shortages of materials, eventually he completed the five hospitals and they were left in operation. Unfortunately through the failure of the Zimbabwe health system, through the countries lack of funds, not through failure of staff only one unit remains operational.

Sadly, the President's wife died, and his residency was revoked. Alan had seen the many needs for pure water and immediately commenced a voluntary position in setting up and maintaining a very practicable ministry of water purification in Zimbabwe, not only there but also the adjoining country of Mozambique, setting up a charity under the name of 'Rivers of Living Water', which hopefully will continue, in the future under God's guidance.

On his return to the UK, Alan trained at Salisbury Cathedral Theological College and became an ordained minister within the URC. It must be said that alongside this commitment he regularly spent time each year in maintaining the large number of units, which he had, installed single-handedly. According to BBC news in 1998 He had saved up to three million lives through the work.

In the last ten years and since the country has suffered severe financial restrictions, which culminated in acute shortages 'Rivers of Living Water' has diversified and to a lesser degree supplied the hospitals with over 300 knitted blankets; Handmade baby clothes; Medicines and donations of children's toys, sweets, along with many other useful donated items. Not just medical establishments but also various orphanages and needy establishments have benefited from its help, including a large school in Matabeleland, and its newest worthy receiver, which has been the 'Mustard Seed' orphanage in Bulawayo.

'Rivers of Living Water' have managed to install water purification plants in the following locations:

1: Bulawayo Mpilo Hospital 8 units
Main pathology lab (2 major motorized units purifying 800 litres an hour along with a UV unit and water softener): 1988 & 2016
Aids Laboratory: 1989
Cancer Unit: 1990
Pharmacy: 1992
Refectory: 1994
Engineering plant: 1994
Main Office and staff quarters: 1995

2: Central hospital Pathology Lab
Main Pathology Lab: 1989 replaced 2018

3: Bulawayo North Ingutsheni hospital
Main Pathology lab: 1998

4: Tsholotsho Hospital
1st Industrial machine in Pathology: 1989

5: St Lukes Hospital Lupane
1st Industrial machine Pathology: 1992

6: Binga Hospital
1st Industrial machine Pathology: 2004-2005

7: Victoria Falls City Hospital
1st machine heavy industrial then replaced: 1990 – 2019

8: Gweru Hospital
1st machine Heavy industrial this was replaced: 1989-2018

9: Kwe Kwe Hospital
1st machine Heavy industrial this was replaced: 1988-2018

10: Chegutu Hospital
1st Machine light industrial: 1990

11: Kadoma Hospital
1st Machine light industrial: 1993

12: Esigodini Hospital
1st Machine light industrial: 1989

13: Gwanda Hospital
1st machine heavy industrial: 1991

13: Masvingo Hospital

1st Machine light industrial: 1998

14: Beitbridge Hospital
1st machine heavy industrial: 1993

Total water purifiers maintained 22. Covering a distance of over 2,000 miles.

Beira Hospital Mozambique, 1 tap for 2,000 patients

Lilian, my wife, giving sweets at Monde school

Mpilo Hospital, presentation water treatment equipment

ACKNOWLEDGEMENTS

This book is not long enough to contain all the wonderful things that have happened during my time in Zimbabwe, or all the magnificent things done for the people of Zimbabwe by individual groups such as 'The Pop Inn' in the Dorset village of Bere Regis where many hundreds of blankets and knitted baby clothes have been donated under the caring direction of Alison Bennett, as well as financial help.

Faithful financing from many churches has been the main source of income, including St Andrews Church, Richmond Hill, Bournemouth; Broadstone United Reformed Church; Throop United Reformed Church; Discovery Church Bournemouth; Rossmore Church, Poole, Dorset: Medstead URC and scores of other churches too numerous to mention. my thanks go to all.

The faithful helpers over the years of the work both here and my friends in Zimbabwe. To mention but a few: Harold Willis, General Secretary; John Hall, Treasurer; Christopher Thomas, Auditor; Les and Margaret Burbidge, Mail distribution; Karen at John Pipe Shippers for allowing my donations to be safely and freely stored, then arranging packing and shipment to Zimbabwe at the best cost to RLW.

Austin Brooke-Thomas who joined me voluntarily over the past three years, learning my trade and sharing the driving, over vast distances of the terrain that we cover.

To my friend of nearly thirty years, Abel Waldman, Chief Technologist, Matabeleland, Zimbabwe. Organising the clearance and storage of shipment from the UK; *(even spending nights in his vehicle to clear the equipment before large costs escalate*). For supplying me a room in his house which still holds my tools and many items I need yearly, and allowing me the freedom of his house since the day it was constructed.

My thanks go to Pastor Philip Chigome and his wife Martha at Hatfield Church, Harare for his care and friendship over the past thirty years.

To the Rev Peter Orton who has become General Secretary and Chairman of 'Rivers of Living Water'.

Finally, and to me the most important contributor is my wife Lilian, who has put up with the many long hours and months of separation, that she has experienced over the years.

Looking after our children and their problems during this period, yet still caring about my work. For without her encouragement and ideas, I could not have faced the task in Southern Africa. With her love and prayers the impossible became possible.

Alan Clarredge

April, 2021

Printed in Great Britain
by Amazon

62106055R00092